Cambridge Elements

Elements in Reinventing Capitalism
edited by
Arie Y. Lewin
Duke University
Till Talaulicar
University of Erfurt

TOWARDS MORE INCLUSIVE VARIETIES OF CAPITALISM

Simon Collinson
Zhejiang University

Shaftesbury Road, Cambridge CB2 8EA, United Kingdom

One Liberty Plaza, 20th Floor, New York, NY 10006, USA

477 Williamstown Road, Port Melbourne, VIC 3207, Australia

314–321, 3rd Floor, Plot 3, Splendor Forum, Jasola District Centre, New Delhi – 110025, India

103 Penang Road, #05–06/07, Visioncrest Commercial, Singapore 238467

Cambridge University Press is part of Cambridge University Press & Assessment, a department of the University of Cambridge.

We share the University's mission to contribute to society through the pursuit of education, learning and research at the highest international levels of excellence.

www.cambridge.org
Information on this title: www.cambridge.org/9781009513609

DOI: 10.1017/9781009513616

© Simon Collinson 2025

This publication is in copyright. Subject to statutory exception and to the provisions of relevant collective licensing agreements, no reproduction of any part may take place without the written permission of Cambridge University Press & Assessment.

When citing this work, please include a reference to the DOI 10.1017/9781009513616

First published 2025

A catalogue record for this publication is available from the British Library

ISBN 978-1-009-51360-9 Hardback
ISBN 978-1-009-51357-9 Paperback
ISSN 2634-8950 (online)
ISSN 2634-8942 (print)

Cambridge University Press & Assessment has no responsibility for the persistence or accuracy of URLs for external or third-party internet websites referred to in this publication and does not guarantee that any content on such websites is, or will remain, accurate or appropriate.

For EU product safety concerns, contact us at Calle de José Abascal, 56, 1°, 28003 Madrid, Spain, or email eugpsr@cambridge.org

Towards More Inclusive Varieties of Capitalism

Elements in Reinventing Capitalism

DOI: 10.1017/9781009513616
First published online: June 2025

Simon Collinson
Zhejiang University

Author for correspondence: Simon Collinson, tsingshanprof02@outlook.com

Abstract: Rising inequality in advanced economies is a global challenge and a major factor behind the current wave of geopolitical disruption. It has been driven by a polarisation between regions that are creating wealth and benefitting from wealth creation, and those left behind. This justifies a wholesale reinvention of these capitalist systems. Focusing on the UK example, this Element presents evidence of systemic failure, with low productivity alongside higher levels of deprivation in city-regions outside of London. Comparisons show that this is a challenge for other advanced economies. Long-term underinvestment in regions has reached a tipping point as a centralised government channels public resources into London, rather than 'levelling-up'. This Element proposes several 'intelligent interventions,' emphasising the need for stronger and more inclusive regional innovation systems, built on a deeper understanding of sustainable local growth pathways. Although based primarily on the UK experience, these policies are relevant beyond the UK context.

This Element also has a video abstract: www.cambridge.org/RECA_Collinson

Keywords: economic growth, capitalism, inequality, inclusive innovation, regional devolution

© Simon Collinson 2025

ISBNs: 9781009513609 (HB), 9781009513579 (PB), 9781009513616 (OC)
ISSNs: 2634-8950 (online), 2634-8942 (print)

Contents

1 Introduction — 1

2 The Signs of Failure — 3

3 The Causes of Failure — 12

4 A Need for Intelligent Intervention — 21

5 Recommendations for New Varieties of Capitalism — 26

6 Conclusions — 42

References — 46

1 Introduction

National economies that have been held up as exemplars of Western capitalism in the past, particularly the UK, are struggling. Alongside a general slowdown in economic growth, the growing polarisation in these advanced economies, between the beneficiaries of these forms of capitalism and disadvantaged communities that are being 'left behind', provides convincing evidence that we need to reinvent capitalism. Recent economic and political shocks have further revealed and worsened these trends, suggesting that 'older' varieties of capitalism are failing to adapt to a new and different global environment. Geopolitical disruption is arguably another symptom of underlying income inequalities. Political elites claim to be supporting deprived communities, focusing on short-term, popularist agendas, but wealth and health inequalities grow.

As a contribution to the 'Reinventing Capitalism' Elements Series, this Element will focus on the failure in the UK capitalist system to manage balanced growth across the economy. It is characterised by highly uneven regional growth rates, with city-regions experiencing persistent low productivity, alongside rising socio-economic inequalities. These in turn underlie disparities in health and welfare across the population, which contribute to the low-growth cycle. Some of the symptoms, the causes and potential solutions to these problems extend beyond the UK example to other advanced liberal democracies, so this Element has a wider relevance to other varieties of capitalism. Slower growth in Europe, particularly in Germany, and very high levels of inequality despite more robust growth in the United States, underpin the rationale for our focus.

Policy interventions to stimulate national and local economic growth, in the UK and elsewhere, have been focused too exclusively on high-growth regions, using current productivity and return-on-investment indicators as the preconditions for further investment and to guide regulation. These performance metrics are also applied in strategies to promote inward foreign direct investment (FDI) and the wider participation of multinational firms in global value chains. Something that has become much more difficult since Brexit, as foreign firms are more attracted to investing in mainland Europe.

This has helped drive the growing polarisation between high-growth and low-growth regions and widening disparities in household incomes and living standards. Such policies are an important focal point because they bridge the public principles and narratives of government with the realities of on-the-ground investments and interventions. These, in turn, shape business investment conditions, and the opportunities open to local communities. They set priorities and privilege one project, place or interest group above others. At the same time, in the UK system, they sit within a wider governance apparatus shaped and managed by a relatively small, centralised group of decision-makers at the heart of the fiscal infrastructure, which directs public spending.

Some of these selection mechanisms and performance metrics that govern public and private resource allocation in these capitalist systems may well be effective in the short term, but they are creating longer-term problems that are undermining the entire system. Long-run productivity in regions outside of London and the South-East of the UK is significantly below expected levels, and low compared with equivalent regions in Europe. A variety of other inequalities, in transport infrastructure, education and skills, household income, and levels of deprivation, health and welfare, match this spatial distribution, as the government fails to address these imbalances or 'level up' the UK economy. This contribution to the Elements Series argues that even if the dominant political agenda supported fundamental reform, the structural mechanisms and governance infrastructures that make up the UK capitalist system are not fit for purpose.

We summarise some of the work conducted at City-REDI, the City-Region Economic Development Institute at the University of Birmingham, to illustrate some of the challenges and solutions. It has a remit to produce the evidence needed to demonstrate how different structural mechanisms, more precise policy interventions and a greater degree of devolution or localisation would be better suited to driving balanced growth (Riley et al., 2022). This requires interdisciplinary analytical approaches for a more holistic understanding of city-regions and the trade-offs between economic growth, social, health and welfare inequalities and the challenges of meeting net-zero targets in complex economic systems. It also requires new methods and tools to evaluate different policy approaches in the context of different places with different challenges and growth opportunities.

Coalitions of local stakeholders should lead new types of interventions with the support of central government, rather than the current system. These have a deeper understanding of local growth opportunities and challenges, and where the consensus lies regarding key priorities. They can also co-opt local organisations that are capable of co-delivering policies and engaging a wider range of local constituencies. This change would help improve the incentives and mechanisms that underlie local inclusive economic growth by more directly connecting the organisations whose role it is to intervene and those communities that would benefit from this improvement. This is a critical component of the reinvention of the UK-type of capitalist system we focus on here.

This contribution to the CUP Elements Series is timely given the impacts of a series of economic shocks on disadvantaged regions in the UK, and the state of UK government. Brexit, COVID-19, the Ukraine war and the emergence of a multi-polar world and trade blocks have revealed structural weaknesses in the UK and other capitalist systems. These are exacerbated by short-term decision-making and self-interested governance. None of the mainstream political parties are able to propose and deliver a broad national direction to galvanise the UK around major national goals. Signs of societal, political and ideological fragmentation, evident in the US, are growing in the UK.

In the following, we briefly review and summarise the empirical evidence that tells us that the capitalist model in the UK is failing (Section 2) and outline the key causes underlying the regional polarisation of wealth and opportunity (Section 3). We then outline how intelligent interventions require better evidence and analysis of how to stimulate local growth opportunities (Section 4) and provide some recommendations for reinventing this model (Section 5), before concluding (Section 6). The work of City-REDI, which has helped reveal some of the symptoms, causes and effects, features throughout. It has also highlighted the scale and seriousness of the challenge.

2 The Signs of Failure

The UK has experienced a significant slowdown in economic growth and lower average levels of productivity, particularly in the last fifteen years. This has evolved alongside, and is directly related to, a significant polarisation between regions that are more productive and create wealth, and those that are less productive, less wealthy and more deprived. For these 'left behind' regions, a simple logic chain goes something like this. They attract lower levels of private investment and are awarded lower levels of public investment. Highly skilled workers are not attracted to the region and/or do not stay in the region. Lower levels of per capita productivity are compounded by periods of rapid deindustrialisation and unemployment as these regions transition away from legacy industries (particularly mining and manufacturing), as described in Section 3 (see the data presented by Stansbury et al., 2023). Weakening regional innovation systems (RIS) are less resilient and adaptive to external shocks or changing economic challenges. Lower skill levels, or the 'wrong skills', increase unemployment and drive down household incomes. This increases deprivation and a dependency on social benefits, lowering health outcomes, pushing up crime levels and overloading public services. The combination of economic and social challenges in such regions makes them much less resilient in the face of economic shocks (more recently, Brexit, COVID-19 and the Ukraine war) widening the gap with regions (particularly London and the South-East) that are more productive and less deprived (Martin et al., 2021; Sensier et al., 2023). Failure, by central and regional governments, to attract foreign investment or compete as a location for high-end activities within global value chains as effectively as in the past has exacerbated these challenges. This sits alongside a weakened entrepreneurial culture, relative to many US states, and smaller economies such as Singapore, Israel or Switzerland.

This (simplified) path-dependent cycle of slow growth, no growth or decline in specific regions reflects not just the economic drivers of unfettered capitalist markets, but also the forms of government intervention in play. Government agencies direct public investment and influence private-sector investment to benefit particular places and socio-economic groups and not others. Rather than 'levelling up' or re-balancing the economy and reducing inequalities, government intervention appears to be having a neutral or even negative impact.

UK regional and urban divides have grown significantly over the last four decades (Carrascal-Incera et al., 2020; Martin et al., 2018; McCann, 2016, 2020). Both wealth and the capacity to create wealth are increasingly concentrated spatially in the UK, and in the USA (Kemeny and Storper, 2023), with some of the same factors that drive differences between national economies driving these regional variations. The economic conditions for growth and for attracting companies, whose success depends on high skilled, high-income workers, are affected by differences in the social, political, legal and institutional contexts across different geographies. Moreover, the polarisation of wealth is mirrored by growing interregional disparities, in household income, skills and knowledge, occupational mobility, health and welfare, as well as in productivity (gross value added (GVA) per capita).

2.1 Productivity

There is general acknowledgement that advanced economies have experienced a slowdown in labour productivity growth since the 2010s, linked to lower (or negative) total factor productivity growth and lower growth in capital per worker hour. The larger, emerging economies, including China and India, are not only growing but also experiencing some of these effects (van Ark et al., 2024).

In terms of economic performance, from 2010 to 2022, the annual average growth in UK GDP per hour was 0.5%. Labour input growth (total hours worked) is projected to slow to 0.3% per year between 2023 and 2035. Relative to its Organisation for Economic Co-operation and Development (OECD) comparators, the UK economy is suffering from persistently low average productivity levels. Failure to increase average productivity growth from 2012–2022 levels would mean that GDP growth from 2023–2035 would be limited to 0.8% per year. To achieve the same GDP growth rate in 2023–2035 as the UK experienced in 1996–2006 would require productivity growth to be raised to 2.2% per year (Coyle et al., 2023, quoting data from the Office for National Statistics).

Average growth levels are constrained by very low productivity in regions outside of London and the South-East of England – a pattern that has emerged in recent decades. Carrascal-Incera et al. (2020) apply a spatial Theil Index to plot the long-run evolution of interregional inequality in GDP per capita across European countries (1900–2010) and point to a U-shaped trend. The UK shows small levels of variation in interregional productivity for nine decades, until 1990 when the growing divergence between regions sets it apart from other countries. By 2010, the UK shows very high interregional differences by international standards. Specifically, the trend lines from 2000 to 2016 show Germany converging and the UK diverging.

Additional data comes from a report for the Industrial Strategy Council in the UK (Zymek and Jones, 2020) showing that the most productive region (West Inner London, one of the wealthiest boroughs) was 70% higher than Northumberland in terms of income per hour. The least productive region, Cornwall in the South-West, was 25% lower than Northumberland. Only eleven out of forty-one NUTS2 regions have productivity higher than the UK average because a small number of high-productivity regions skew the average productivity statistics. The gap between the UK regions with the highest and lowest productivity is bigger than the equivalent gaps in Germany, France, Italy and Spain. But it is the case that regional divergence is occurring in a wider range of countries, just to a lesser extent than in the UK (Gómez-Tello, Murgui-García and Sanchis-Llopis, 2020). Education and skills, alongside the state of RIS, are part of the underlying dynamics of this weakness.

2.2 Education and Skills

Education and skills have a significant impact on firm-level productivity and performance, which underpins economic growth and wealth creation at the regional level. The share of the population with a tertiary education correlates significantly with regional productivity, as does the share with a secondary qualification (Coyle, et al., 2023). Some studies suggest that this correlation can explain 'mechanically' much of the average income differences between regions (Overman and Xu, 2022).

But education and skills also represent a critical link, via employment and salaries, to household income, which determines relative levels of deprivation, socio-economic equality and community resilience. Inequalities in education attainment levels and skills by region contribute to regional differences in wealth creation, income distribution and household deprivation across the UK (and most economies).

The UK generally has seen investment in education decline, with spending as a share of national income falling from 5.6% in 2010–2011 to 4.4% in 2022–2023 (Drayton et al., 2024). Total adult skills spending in 2024–2025 is expected to be 23% below 2009–2010 levels. 33.8%, or 16.4 million people aged sixteen years and over in England and Wales had Level 4 or higher-level qualifications, including Higher National Certificate, Higher National Diploma, Bachelor's degree or post-graduate qualifications in 2021. 18.2% (8.8 million) are reported as having no qualifications. London, with 46.7% (3.3 million), has the highest percentage of the population in the UK with Level 4 or above qualifications. Moreover, this unequal distribution and the socio-economic inequalities in education and skills generally, have worsened since the COVID-19 pandemic (Blundell et al., 2020).

When we focus on the later stages of pre-employment education, the share of eighteen-year-olds who are 'not in education, employment or training' (known as NEETs) reached 16% in 2022, close to the levels seen in economic recession of the late 2000s. Around a third of young people have completed all of their education by the age of eighteen, compared to 20% in France and Germany (Thwaites and Try, 2023). Blundell et al. (2021) also describe big differences in the proportion of people with or without post A-level qualifications across the country. In many places, less than a quarter of the population have post A-level qualifications, but in large parts of London, the South and South-East of England, almost half of the people have a post A-level education.

Some commentary notes that disadvantaged areas receive higher levels of spending for students in further education (FE) colleges, up to 9% higher in the most deprived areas than in the wealthiest areas. However, these account for 5% of UK students. For the other 95% in higher education (HE) funding is unequally distributed and favours wealthier regions. In terms of the area that students come from, HE-spending per young person is highest in London (£15,800) and lowest in Northamptonshire (£5,800) and Blackpool (£6,250) (Drayton et al., 2024). This is due to spatial differences in university participation rates, with young people from wealthier areas more likely to attend higher education.

The distribution of education levels relates to other kinds of inequality. This includes wages and wider measures of deprivation. A slightly dated but very robust study by Gibbons et al. (2013) found that 90% of the differences in area-level wages can be explained by differences in the dispersion of highly skilled workers. Similarly, Davenport and Zaranko (2020) use four variables to generate a 'left behind' index and find that the 'share of individuals with a degree' is more unequally dispersed than 'incapacity benefit claimants', 'employment' and 'wage levels', but all are related. Agrawal and Philips (2020) draw on UK Department for Education data to link the percentage of young people going to higher education by region and Free School Meal status, which is used as a proxy measure of deprivation by many studies.

2.3 Regional Innovation Systems

Skills and productivity are strongly connected to RIS and agglomerations or clusters of economic growth. Strong RIS provide resilience and adaptability in the face of external shocks as well as underpinning high-productivity economic activities in sectors such as automotive and aerospace manufacturing, pharmaceuticals and software development. There is a strong consensus that research and development (R&D) activity boosts general productivity in regions (Aitken et al., 2021; Coyle et al., 2023; Griffith et al., 2006) and that public R&D investments 'crowd-in' private investment (Aitken et al., 2021; Moretti et al., 2019). There is also strong evidence that public and private R&D investment together create localised spillover effects, benefitting both productivity levels and RIS more generally. Moreover, universities act as a strong catalyst for these spillovers (Kantor and Whalley, 2014), via both the funding of R&D directly and investments in RIS commercialisation mechanisms such as technology transfer agencies (Collinson, 2020; Hausman, 2022; Johnston et al., 2022). Innovation is also key to improving sustainability and reaching net-zero targets, but sometimes with the cost of lowering productivity. Different innovation strategies or business models can lead to more or less inclusivity through impacts on employment and wage levels. We examine some of these policy trade-offs in Section 5.

In 2020, the UK spent 2.93% of GDP on R&D. Businesses fund just under 60% (£38.7 billion in 2021) and perform just over 70% (£46.9 billion) of R&D, while the public sectors fund 19% (£12.8 billion) and perform 5% (£3.4 billion). Higher education institutions, primarily the research-intensive universities, are key in that they fund 8% (£5.6 billion) but perform 25% (£14.9 billion) of R&D (Panjwani, 2023).

The evidence shows that specific areas of discretionary government R&D funding, including direct public R&D expenditure and higher education R&D, are heavily skewed towards already productive and wealthier regions. Direct government R&D expenditure in 2016 was £60 per capita in London and the South-East of England, but only £21 in the North of England, £14 in the Midlands, and £7 and £5 in Northern Ireland and Wales, respectively (Forth and Jones, 2020). More recent public R&D funding data, using a different definition (so not directly comparable), shows that 52% of the total in 2021 was spent in London, the East and South-East of England (£34.4 billion). This amounts to £1,406 per person, which is well above the UK average of £987 per person, and contrasts to £534 of R&D funding per person in Wales (46% below the UK average) (Panjwani, 2023). At least part of the reason for this concentration is that many leading research-intensive universities are based in London or in the 'golden triangle' linking the capital city with Oxford and Cambridge. But this illustrates the 'catch-22' cycle of reinvestment in more productive places, which underlies the spatial polarisation we are discussing (Collinson et al., 2023a).

Comparisons with the United States are generally incomplete, but they do suggest that success in attracting high-end investment, particularly R&D-intensive assets to 'peripheral regions', can be partly attributed to significant state-level support, including tax breaks and subsidies. Co-investment by central government can also pump-prime wider effects. The Research Triangle Park in North Carolina, for example, originally attracted IBM, Burroughs Welcome and others alongside government laboratories such as EPA NIEHS. There are similar success stories in Tennessee and Texas and more recently Arizona.

Germany provides a more useful comparator, in that public sector and higher education R&D investments are explicitly targeted at less-well-off places to counteract regional economic inequalities. The UK's approach has tended to worsen these inequalities. Moreover, there is evidence that city-regions such as Manchester and Birmingham have much higher potential to link university-based R&D with local absorptive capacity, given the large hinterland of firms across a wide range of sectors (compared to Oxford or Cambridge, for example). Birmingham, in the West Midlands, attracts disproportionately more private R&D investment than public investment, suggesting a difference between the market drivers for locating R&D activities and the selection mechanisms for targeting public R&D resource allocation (Forth and Jones, 2020).

2.4 Income, Assets and Wealth

In terms of income and deprivation, the spatial distribution patterns match those of high and low economic growth and productivity. Geary and Stark (2016) show that the South-East has been the richest region of the UK since at least the 1860s, though regional inequalities reduced gradually between the 1860s and the 1970s, since when they have increased again. In *Capital in the 21st Century*, Thomas Piketty (2014) also takes a long-term view using data on income distribution for the US and European countries (including the UK) between 1910 and 2010. This shows a U-shaped curve of decreasing and then increasing inequality for all countries, but one that is particularly pronounced for the UK and even more so for the United States. At the start and end of this trend line, the top 10% of US earners receive 50% of total incomes. The relative Gini coefficients show a worsening trend in recent decades, and the inequality of income distribution in the United States now is fairly similar to that of Tanzania and Peru, for example. Piketty's seminal work has been criticised and even contradicted (e.g. Hudson and Tribe, 2017), but it triggered a stream of work on the topic, including many more fine-grained and sophisticated empirical studies.

A robust, systematic comparison of spatial wage disparities 'between and within similarly defined local labour market areas (LLMAs)' for Canada, France, Germany, the UK, and the United States between 1975 and 2019 is conducted by Bauluz et al. (2023). By the end of this period, spatial inequalities in average wages across these LLMAs are similar in Canada, France, Germany and the UK, whereas the United States exhibits the highest degree of spatial inequality. However, they have nearly doubled in all these countries, over the forty years analysed, except for France where they are closer to 1970s levels. Notably, this study suggests that the contribution of spatial geography or place in explaining national wage inequality has stayed constant in all except in the UK where there is a significant increase.

Real wages grew by 33% each decade from 1970 to 2007 in the UK, but low or no growth since 2007 has worsened income inequality. As a result, UK households are 9% poorer on average than French counterparts and 27% poorer for low-income families. In 2019, income per person in the wealthiest local authority (Kensington and Chelsea) was £52,500, over four times that of the poorest, which was Nottingham at £11,700 (Thwaites and Try, 2023).

Household wealth, which accounts for assets (including house ownership), savings and investments, is perhaps a better general indicator (than income) of inequality and relative resilience in the face of economic shocks. In the United States, this has now reached a level whereby an estimated 67% of wealth is owned by the top 10% of earners, with the lowest 50% of earners owning 2.5% (Sullivan, Hays and Bennett, 2023). In the UK, 43% of wealth in the UK is owned by top 10% of earners and the lowest 50% of earners own 9% (ONS, 2022). Some of Piketty's detailed explanation is summarised in Section 3. Separate studies have identified a similar pattern in emerging economies, notably China (Dunford, 2022). As in the US example, growth rates are stronger than the global average, but inequalities are also growing faster.

2.5 Poverty, Social Mobility and Health

By one definition, 22% or 14.4 million people in the UK were in poverty in 2021/2022. The West Midlands had the highest rate at 27%, followed by the North-East, Yorkshire and The Humber, the East Midlands and the North-West. But also, near the top sits London at 25%, standing out from the least-poor regions of the South of England. As by far the largest city in the UK, London combines the most productive and wealthiest, with some of the poorest in the country (JRF, 2024).

The poorest places are also those regions with the lowest levels of social mobility and opportunity, indicating the likelihood of moving out of poverty into higher-income socio-economic groups. Out of the twenty-four at the bottom of the list, twenty-one are in the North (East and West), Yorkshire and The Humber, and the Midlands (East and West). London, the South-East and the South dominate the rankings of the most socially mobile areas and only three are in the above regions (Social Mobility Commission, 2020). So, despite having some of the poorest neighbourhoods in the country, Londoners have a much higher level of social mobility relative to counterparts in other regions.

Average mortality rates for men and women in England are now worse than most European counterparts (although not Poland, for example), but better than the United States. Again, the regional distribution patterns described earlier in this Section also apply to mortality rates and general health data across the UK. Male life expectancy in England in 2020 was 10.3 years (8.3 years for females) shorter in the most deprived areas (Glasgow for the UK and Blackpool for England) compared to the least deprived (Islington, London). This gap was a full year larger compared to 2019 because of COVID-19, which exacerbated existing health inequalities. However, this is still the largest health inequality gap recorded by Public Health England after over two decades of comparable records. Although COVID-19 contributed significantly as a major cause of death in 2020, higher mortality rates from heart disease, lung cancer and chronic lower respiratory diseases in deprived areas were still important contributors (Public Health England, 2024). Other barriers to social mobility follow this distribution including the prevalence of mental illness, learning and other disabilities, obesity and diabetes.

2.6 Connecting Wealth Creation and Wealth Distribution

When we integrate data and evidence connecting spatial and socio-economic inequalities in a systematic way, we can see the significance of these trends in terms of the growing pressure on society and political systems in capitalist economies. A widely cited analysis by McCann (2020; McCann and Ortega-Argilés, 2021; McCann et al., 2021) gave rise to the term 'the geography of discontent' linking economic, social and political polarisation across the UK following Brexit, and later COVID-19. This concludes that the UK is 'almost certainly the most inter-regionally unequal large high-income country' on the basis of twenty-eight measures of regional economic inequality compared across industrialised economies. He also concludes that the UK's interregional inequality is particularly notable given that it occurs over small geographic distances.

McCann (2020) shows that relative to counterparts, the UK is in the top half for all twenty-eight measures, is in the top quarter for twenty-one of the twenty-eight measures and is the most unequal on five of the twenty-eight measures. These are: (1) GDP per capita, ratio of highest-to-lowest OECD TL3 regions; (2) GDP per capita divided by national GDP per capita, taking the difference between the highest and lowest OECD TL3 area; (3) RDI (regional disposable income) per person, taking the ratio of highest-to-lowest 20% across OECD TL3 regions; (4) Gini index of regional GDP per capita across OECD TL3 regions; (5) Gini index of regional RDI per capita across OECD TL3 regions. The comparison shows that the United States is more unequal than the UK on five measures, and the UK is more inter-regionally unequal than the United States on six measures (which we can 'score' as 6–5), while they are equal on two measures. Similar comparisons with other OECD countries show that the UK is more unequal than the following countries: Spain 3–19, Japan 0–18, Germany 4–17, South Korea 2–16, France 4–15 and Italy 10–11.

McCann and colleagues make the empirical link between low productivity and inequality. Much of this is reaffirmed and extended in a detailed analysis by Stansbury et al. (2023), who conclude that the UK's current 'regional economic inequality problem is primarily a productivity problem' rather than an (un) employment problem, which was a key factor in previous periods such as the 1980s. They map productivity differences between London and the South-East against other regions (including Europe) using comparisons of population-weighted coefficient of variation in regional GVA per worker. The underperformance of most city-regions outside of London is a key focus. These cities, and Manchester and Birmingham in particular, 'do not appear to benefit from the agglomeration economies seen in other industrialised countries, where scale and population density are strongly associated with higher productivity' (McCann and Yuan, 2022; Rossi et al., 2023). This analysis also points to historical periods of rapid deindustrialisation, relative to counterparts in the South-East of England and across Europe. But while education and skills are a factor affecting both productivity and income differentials, 'there is still a large regional productivity gap even controlling for education'.

3 The Causes of Failure

Prior analyses of capitalism (and there are a lot) commonly emphasise the need to understand the system as a whole. But it is a complex adaptive system at any scale (firm, sector, region, nation) with a wide variety of relationships between many components, with both the components and the relationships changing rapidly. Moreover, the lack of an understanding of how individual or combined interventions impact many parts of this system is a contributing factor behind the failure of many policy interventions (Balland, et al., 2022).

The excellent 'Varieties of Capitalism' (Hall and Soskice, 2001) provides a framework for understanding how and why capitalist systems vary around the world and has led to further systemic research on these combined effects. Differences across five 'spheres', industrial relations, vocational training and education, corporate governance, inter-firm relations and relations with employees, underpin distinctive types of capitalist system. Writing some time ago, the authors also proposed that liberal market economies (such as the United States, UK, Canada, Australia, New Zealand, Ireland) tend to distribute income and employment more unequally than coordinated market economies (e.g. Germany, France, Japan). The institutional arrangements of a nation's political economy tend to push its companies towards particular kinds of corporate strategy and innovation, and so help explain different models of wealth creation. But these forms of institutional, financial and governance structures are also important determinants of wealth distribution, underpinning path dependencies that help concentrate wealth in particular groups and places.

In a subsequent analysis, Hall and Gingerich (2009) construct indices to assess whether patterns of coordination in the OECD economies conform to the predictions of the theory and compare the correspondence of institutions across sub-spheres of the political economy. Differences in shareholder power, dispersion of control, size of stock market, level of wage coordination, degree of wage coordination and labour turnover help explain differences in wealth distribution. More recent research has built on this to add further insights into economic growth and inequality (Behringer and van Treeck, 2022; Movahed, 2023).

In *Capital in the 21st Century*, Thomas Piketty (2014) maps long-term patterns of economic growth over periods of both convergence and divergence of incomes and well-being across households in different nations. His overarching conclusion is that the 'rapid accumulation and concentration of wealth allowing top earners to separate themselves from the majority' can continue 'even when all conditions of market efficiency for economists are satisfied'. Specifically relevant to the current trends in the US and UK economies (which are Piketty's key examples), 'even when low growth dominates, return on capital can be high but only benefits the wealthy'. He points to the diffusion of knowledge and skills as the most important force in favour of greater equality, and something that does not happen automatically.

Several factors help explain this growing polarisation. Piketty suggests that top managers have either increased their productivity relative to that of other workers or, more likely, are able to set their own wages 'without limit and without connection to productivity'. Perhaps more significantly in the current era, private wealth accumulation in terms of real estate (particularly in the UK), financial assets, and professional capital net of debt all takes on a disproportionate weighting at times of slow growth and when wages lag inflation. This drives divergence.

Economists and management theorists have also noted the dangers and imperfections with capitalist models for a long time. As noted by Diane Coyle (2023), Adam Smith famously noted the risks as well as advocating the benefits of the dynamism of increasing specialisation. Collusion among producers at the expense of consumers undermined competition and allowed the benefits of wealth creation to be captured by those with market power. Others have noted similar tendencies within evolving business models as we have '... transitioned into the era of financialization, with shareholder value replacing customer value as the purpose of the corporation, leaving managers to divert resources to their own enrichment and that of shareholders, at the expense of investment in future innovation' (Denning and Hastings, 2024).

Before looking more closely at the UK experience, Spain provides an interesting, brief example of a successful 'turnaround' economy. As one of the original European laggards, it suffered from slow GDP growth and very weak wage growth for many decades, until recently. In 2024, Spain's GDP grew by 3.2%, which was about five times the eurozone average growth rate and more than the United States. A successful tourism industry, strong public investment (partly helped by the EU's COVID pandemic recovery funding), increased services and industrial exports to the European single market, a stronger financial services and technology sector, and low energy costs due to investment in renewables, have driven this growth. Immigration has also brought in cheaper labour, but unemployment has declined. Productivity, however, has remained low relative to the OECD average (OECD, 2024).

Importantly, despite the influx of lower-paid immigrant labour, wage inequality has improved in Spain. Left-leaning governments since 2018 have strengthened wage-setting institutions, collective bargaining, employment protection and job retention support. Spain has also significantly increased its minimum wage (by over 50%) to promote a broader sharing of productivity gains with workers, particularly those with low wages. The minimum wage level was raised in 2019 and again more recently. This has increased the wages of directly affected workers by almost 6%, while (contrary to economists' predictions) it reduced employment by only 0.6% (OECD, 2024). It may be a bit too early to tell, but this could be an example of strong government intervention triggering both high growth and reduced income polarisation, without impacting productivity levels.

3.1 UK-Specific Challenges

Alongside the general difficulties described in Section 2, the UK faces additional challenges, many of which are related to regional imbalances (Pike et al., 2016). Three have been identified recently by Coyle, van Ark and Pendrill (2023). The first is long-term underinvestment in the economy, referring to physical, human and intangible capital, public and private investment. UK companies have invested 20% less than those in the United States, France and Germany since 2005 (public investment is discussed in Section 3.2). This puts Britain in the bottom 10% of OECD countries and is estimated to have cost 4% of GDP (Thwaites and Try, 2023). This reflects both public-sector and private-sector choices and incentives. Second, the inadequate diffusion of productivity-enhancing practices between firms and places, despite world-leading science and technology. Third, institutional fragmentation and a lack of joined-up policies partly related to the centralisation of decision-making in London and the fragmented nature of governance structures elsewhere.

Dealing with each of these challenges benefits from a place-based approach as all three are negatively impacting regions outside of London and the South-East of England. This can also help reveal differences in the (sub-)varieties of capitalism operating at a local level, providing a better understanding of their distinctive challenges and the types of customised policy interventions needed to tackle these.

Aspects of both 'localisation economies' and 'urbanisation economies' appear to be failing to fully operate in some large UK city-regions outside of London. The former, also termed Marshallian externalities, are the agglomeration benefits that firms experience from being located near to many other similar firms, including access to skills and knowledge. The latter, also known as 'Jacobs externalities', stem from the proximity of many firms from different sectors in urban centres, providing access to a range of skills and knowledge and a pool of clients and consumers (Rossi et al., 2023).

Following an economic growth diagnostic approach developed by Hausmann, Rodrik, and Velasco (2008; and Hausmann, Klinger and Wagner, 2008), several studies identify 'binding constraints' on regional growth. These aim to isolate factors that are key targets for effective policy interventions. After discounting some factors, Stansbury et al. (2023) find evidence that the following are key: a relative shortage of STEM degrees; binding transport infrastructure constraints within major non-London conurbations; a failure of public innovation policy to support clusters beyond the South-East, in particular through the regional distribution of public support for R&D; missed opportunities for higher internal mobility due to London's overheating housing market. They subsequently focus on four key policy levers in the areas of education, infrastructure, support for R&D and access to finance.

In the UK, wealth accumulation through ownership of assets, notably house ownership, but also stock market and pensions investments, have helped drive polarisation. Those without assets experience a growing reliance on short-term earn–spend cycles and debt accumulation locks deprived communities in 'left behind' regions. Successive economic shocks (Brexit, COVID and Ukraine) have had a greater impact on low-income regions outside London and South-East England, particularly those with a higher dependence on manufacturing industries and the movement of physical goods. There is also some evidence that quantitative easing led by the UK government during and after the COVID pandemic indirectly helped wealthier places and/or households (Sensier et al., 2023).

Structural embeddedness and path dependency are also influenced by the longer-term effects of deindustrialisation on particular regions. Stansbury, Turner and Balls (2023) cite data from the EU ARDECO dataset mapping the biggest ten-year periods of deindustrialisation across all EU regions, 1980–2019 in terms of a 'change in employment share' (ranging from –0.1 to –0.17). With the transition from legacy industry sectors, especially mining and manufacturing, to financial and creative services, for example, regions across Europe experienced significant decline and pressure to restructure. This was partly related to their initial level of dependence on a specific industry sector in decline (i.e. not so 'smart specialisation' in retrospect) as well as the growth potential in other sectors. Three German regions, Sachsen-Anhalt, Sachsen and Thüringen, top this table, but only appear once, for the 1991–2001 decade. Any (NUTS2) region in Europe can be listed more than once, for each subsequent decade that a high level of change in employment share occurred. The key point for us is that sixteen out of the thirty-one regions listed are in the Midlands (nine in the West and seven in the East Midlands) and twenty in the UK (Stansbury, Turner and Balls, 2023, table 1, P.65).

The term 'development traps' has been used to describe places that get stuck in persistent low-growth or stagnation, often linked to an extended dependence on legacy industries (mining and manufacturing in the UK case) and failure to transition into new growth sectors. Some studies emphasise a lack of capabilities to develop high-complexity activities in regions with industry structures that are dominated by low-complexity economic activities. This sits within a broader evolutionary framing that analyses regional differences in terms of the local mix, complexity and relatedness of industry activities (or industry portfolio) associated with 'smart specialisation' policy approaches (Balland et al., 2019, 2022; Iammarino et al., 2019; Pinheiro et al., 2022).

At the same time, a number of factors benefit London and the South-East to drive further wealth polarisation. The concentration of asset wealth (particularly property ownership and pensions), supported by increased house prices, sits alongside higher levels of disposable income and consumption, which creates stronger multipliers benefitting local goods and service providers. This is partly a result of where the wealthy live and spend their income, but also results from the economics of agglomeration that benefit places that are home to the largest or the most productive firms. In Keynesian terms, localised aggregate demand externalities benefit some places and not others, for considerable periods without market interventions. Because large agglomerations also benefit disproportionately from investment and spending that takes place elsewhere, via national value chains, London benefits more than any other city-region from economic activity and added value wherever it is created across the country.

Some of the same factors are driving the polarisation in other countries. As noted by Kemeny and Storper (2023), the significant increase in spatial inequality in the United States, particularly since 1980, is mainly driven by a small number of 'resiliently high-income superstar city-regions'. Competition between states and cities has increased, but many US states have still managed to attract or stimulate entrepreneurship, and the overall national growth rate has been stronger than the UK's. Perhaps this makes the increased inequality in the United States less noticeable.

A final driver is public spending and investment, which privileges London and the South-East both through subsidies to reduce the 'natural' market costs of agglomeration, for example, through very high per capita funding for transport. But also, through higher levels of support for education and low-income communities compared to other UK city-regions. The cycle of attraction, central to market economies, whereby private investment and high-skilled, high-income workers tend to concentrate in increasingly prosperous city-regions, is intensified in the current political system by incentives for public investment, which prioritise the most productive places (Collinson et al., 2023a; Newman et al., 2023). This is examined more thoroughly in the following section.

Arguably, as the capacity of the UK economy to create value has declined, mechanisms that enable value appropriation by smaller numbers of (spatially clustered) people have become more prevalent. At the same time, central government has directed public-sector spending to boost the most successful regions and underfunded the others. The point is not only that this is unfair or immoral; it is not sustainable, in economic or political terms.

3.2 Regional Governance Structures and Public Spending Patterns

In terms of tax raising and spending powers, and many other areas of governance, the UK is one of the most centralised governments of any advanced economy. It has a smaller number of sub-regions with local governance structures, overseeing relatively large number of inhabitants. Moreover, on average and compared to OECD counterparts, these sub-national government bodies have the responsibility for investing a much lower proportion of public expenditure than central government.

The OECD breaks down sub-national governments into three levels: municipal (the UK has 374), intermediary (35) and regional or state level (three, being England, Scotland and Wales). The average size of a 'municipality' in the UK is 180,564 people compared to an average for the thirty-eight OECD countries of 10,016. The average number of municipalities per 100,000 inhabitants in the UK is 0.6, compared to an OECD average of 10.0. Only Korea and Ireland are similar in having a small number of sub-regions with large populations. Public expenditure accounts for 48.6% of GDP in the UK (the OECD average is 45.5%) and the sub-national government investment as a proportion of public investment overall is 28.8% in the UK compared to an OECD average of 54.5% (OECD, 2023a).

In parallel with these patterns of spending, the scale of central government, partly indicated by the proportion of civil service employees based in London, has grown while declining in every other English region. One estimate shows that the civil service headcount in London increased by 22% between 2010 and 2022 and by almost 8% in Wales and 1% in Scotland (as devolved governments) but fell by over 30% in some other English regions during this period. Central government in the UK now employs more people than at any time in its past while local government employment is at its lowest point since 1963 (Forth, 2023).

Alongside a highly centralised governance structure controlling public spending, we note significant imbalances in the proportion of public spending going to different regions. Data on education, skills and public R&D investments are presented in Sections 2.2 and 2.3. Alongside these, housing and transport infrastructure are underpinning factor endowments that support local economic growth. Moreover, public investments in these and other endowments and amenities can 'crowd in' private-sector investment and stimulate wider multiplier effects (Crafts, 2009; Vasilakos et al., 2023).

Transport provides a clear illustration of both an overall decline in investment and a strong regional bias in government support. Transport infrastructure investment as a share of GDP overall has been low in the UK by international standards. UK cities outside of London have less extensive and less reliable public transport networks than other Western European cities. Taking into account population differences, 'the share of the total city population that can reach the city centre within 30 minutes by public transport is 23 percentage points lower in the UK's cities than in Western Europe' (Coyle et al., 2023). Data on total public transport investments across regions shows that since 2010 £1,500 per person has been spent in North England compared to £3,000 per person in the South-East of England and £6,000 per person in London (Coyle et al., 2023; Forth, 2023). Alongside this, lower housing density in UK cities amounts to weaker agglomeration economies, including lower levels of accessibility to available jobs in city centres for lower-income households (Rodrigues and Breach, 2021). Further analysis and empirical evidence describing the interregional imbalance in public investment and spending and outlining some of the causes and implications are in Newman et al. (2023) and Collinson et al. (2022).

The 'Green Book' investment evaluation and appraisal process, which is a set of procedural guidelines used by Treasury and other government departments to assess the benefit–cost ratio or trade-offs for a public investment proposal, is an important example. At the general level, and acknowledged now by Treasury, the approach is too focused on measurable monetary quantities in terms of value for money at local, regional and national levels. A mechanistic modelling approach habitually leaves out social value and other contextual factors for which there are no market prices. It is also applied in attempts to measure likely outcomes when the complexity of causal linkages is too great for reductionist models.

More specifically, economic growth investment appraisals guided by Green Book have tended to take productivity (GVA per capita) as the main, or only, indicator of success. As such, regions with the highest potential to improve productivity with investment in factor endowments like transport infrastructure, housing, education or R&D assets have received the most funding from central government. These are the regions with already high levels of productivity, and superior factor endowments, that is, London and the greater South-East of

England (Brown, 2023; Coyle and Sensier, 2020; Mealy and Coyle, 2022). This is part of a wider, entrenched path dependency created by a policy regime that privileges places that are more productive, rather than enabling growth in lagging regions. It is embedded in the political economy of the country and in the selection mechanisms for resource allocation, or wealth distribution, across the country. These are important 'rules of the game' that maintain imbalances that need to be reversed.

Some would say that these rules of the game are politically motivated by an entrenched elite that uses them to maintain privileged access to the mechanisms of rent appropriation. Clear evidence for this is difficult to find or build, partly because of the indistinct nature and increased 'churn' in the members of the controlling elite. But the evidence does show a more centralised government, with more civil service employees and elected leaders based in London, plus patterns of investment strongly preferring London and the South-East. As indicated throughout this Section, both political structures and economic patterns need to be understood in tandem to provide insights into socio-economic inequalities. It is important to both distinguish and to connect political agendas (which can be short-lived or persistent), institutional and governance infrastructures for raising and spending public finance (which tend to evolve and become path-dependent), and market forces. The latter act across a changing geography of investment and disinvestment as capital and skills move around, influenced more or less by policy interventions.

Structural weaknesses in the UK capitalist system are now being revealed and exacerbated by short-term decision-making, rapidly changing policy agendas and weak governance under successive national governments. Policy churn and short termism, relative to both other advanced economies and the UK in the past, have been noted in a number of studies (Westwood et al., 2022). This has undermined the economic resilience and worsened the impact of recent economic shocks on some places, alongside the effects of long-term specialisation in lagging industry sectors (Qamar et al., 2022; Sensier et al., 2023). The spatial geography of these impacts and subsequent increases in polarisation between the 'haves and have nots' provides a useful framing, following the 'geography of discontent' across UK regions (McGann and Ortega-Argiles, 2021).

The concentration and centralisation of decision-making power over the allocation of public resources, the lack of devolution and the presence of 'weak institutions' outside of the centre compound these challenges (Collinson et al., 2023a; Rodríguez-Pose and Muštra, 2022). The mechanisms of metagovernance present structural challenges to the 'levelling up' agenda that the country needs. A complex and ineffective mix of quasi-market approaches, like the Green Book approach, and the continual reinforcement of state hierarchies, with different flavours brought in by successive political leaders, prevents the development of local sovereignty (Fransham et al., 2023; Tomaney and Pike, 2020). Restrictions around local government activity significantly constrain local capacity to build public–private coalitions to deliver economic development in the 'left behind' regions (Coyle and Muhtar, 2023; Lumpkin et al., 2024; Newman et al., 2023).

At the time of writing this, the stark change of leadership in the United States with the embedding of President Trump and acolytes into a wide range of governance structures is partly driven by perceptions of systemic bias in previous administrations. The new regime is certainly embarked on a wholesale restructuring of the government apparatus, from new targeted outcomes to incentive structures, funding mechanisms, the allocation of decision-making power, radical shake-ups of the administration and its practices, alongside changes to the federal relationship with individual states, and a fundamental reboot in relations with other nation states. Salter (2024) in a contribution to this Element series directly comments on this change and the need for greater political equality, underpinned by reciprocity and power sharing. It is too soon to see where this might lead, but any reduction in the current level of socio-economic inequality in the United States seems highly unlikely at this stage. The opposite seems the more probable outcome.

We might ask whether this type of radical political solution could support positive change in the UK context. There do seem to be fewer scenarios in the UK context where this radical type of political change seems viable, but 'never say never'. The real question, given the central concerns of this Element, is whether such a power shift and/or a fundamental change in the style of government could trigger a significant improvement in both productivity and socio-economic equality in the UK. The answer is probably yes, at least as regards the latter, a major transformation in the structure, style and mechanisms of government, is a requirement. The current government has made policy changes with some of these targets in mind but once again does not appear to be changing enough of basic structural conditions that underpin the the range of challenges presented here. As described throughout this Element, the problems facing the UK are so entrenched, long-term and path dependent that a turnaround requires something new.

Putting politics and the wider considerations to one side, we return to the more limited scope of this Element. Regardless of the kind of governance regime in place, a specific set of practical policy interventions are needed to tackle the challenges outlined in Section 3. The next section (Section 4) describes why and how these need to be 'intelligent interventions'. Precisely targeted investments and intercessions that are going to leverage very limited resources to engineer significant change need to be based on data, evidence and intelligence.

4 A Need for Intelligent Intervention

Policymaking is a complex (imperfect, organic, contested) selection environment, and successive UK governments have been failing to invest in the right ways and in the right places for long-term balanced (inclusive) economic growth. A wider range of changes need to be made than we can capture in this Element. We could focus on agency and incentive structures that have supported the concentration of wealth, particularly asset ownership, or the selection environment responsible for directing politicians to allocate public resources in ways that have increased inequalities. But we chose to focus on a specific subset of practical recommendations in this section and the next (Section 5).

Policy interventions that have any chance of improving the development pathways of regions trapped in low-growth cycles need to be precise and customised for the challenges and growth potential of these regions. Currently, there are gaps in, and between, (1) data on the symptoms and evidence of specific areas of failure in capitalist systems, (2) a comprehensive understanding of the underlying causes of failure, and (3) feasible, realistic options for selectively intervening in different parts of these economic systems to improve the outcomes. More generally, a gap exists between well-meaning but naïve calls focused on the 'destruction of capitalism', and practical but path-breaking changes to put economic systems on better growth trajectories.

Much of the public narrative is grandiose and idealistic, calling for a wholesale change in the values and behaviours of corporations, consumers and political leaders. This may well be needed, but it will not happen without real-world changes to the incentive structures and selection mechanisms that underlie their behaviours. Alongside the evangelising, among the growing number of studies on corporate social responsibility and ethical capitalism, this gap is now being filled with more insightful analyses. Selected writings are starting to bridge high-level proselytising about culture, trust and values with interventions that are based on real-world evidence of the problems and potential solutions.

For example, a recent book by Lavie (2023) calling for a cooperative economy, which initially appears to be overly idealistic, does provide ideas for some intelligent interventions. The 'ideal' is 'an ethical community-driven exchange system that relies on collective action ('prosocial behaviour') to promote societal values while accounting for resource constraints . . .' and 'moves away from a materialistic orientation, limiting overconsumption and excessive profit-making'. All obviously desirable, but in explaining the design principles for a cooperative economy, more realistic, evidenced interventions to enhance economic equality are outlined. These include the use of price subsidisation, effective barriers to prevent the emergence of monopoly platforms, and legally limiting disparities in income and wealth accumulation.

Another analysis, 'The Profiteers' (Marquis, 2024), clearly and helpfully articulates how firms have managed to privatise, or ring-fence, profits and the rewards from wealth creation while socialising or externalising the 'costs of environmental damage, low wages, systemic discrimination, and cheap goods'. This provides clear targets and mechanisms for intervening, underpinned by a strong understanding of how firms have been able to limit their own exposure to the full social and environmental costs of economic activity to maximise profits. It also comes with a starting point for change in the form of the 'B Lab' certification process committing companies to putting the rights of workers, community impact, social benefits and environmental stewardship on an equal footing with financial shareholders (Marquis, 2020). This sits alongside other contributions that seek to understand the trade-offs between shareholder- and stakeholder-driven structures, and private-sector versus government-mandated solutions to social problems (Holmes et al., 2022). For many authors, a core aim is to address the declining trust in capitalism, which could lead to less intelligent interventions and significantly worse future outcomes, driven by short-term political ambition and/or 'mob rule' through social media.

A final example comes from the work of Mazzucato, who is known as an advocate of mission-driven economic change with innovation at the heart of growth, and government taking a key role (Mazzucato, 2021; Mazzucato and Perez, 2023). A deep understanding of innovation systems and the historical success and failure of related government interventions through time and across various national contexts underpins this analysis and helps to connect grand macro-level shifts with practical tools for driving change. Mazzucato also adds robustness by applying policy evaluation approaches to estimate fiscal multipliers and crowding-in effects, for example, from private investment in R&D (Deleidi and Mazzucato, 2021). This provides a link to the work of City-REDI, as does a shared belief that 'without smart government at the organisational level, smart (innovation-led) growth is impossible'.

From these accounts, it is clear that targeted interventions that are going to leverage limited resources to engineer significant change need to be based on data, evidence and intelligence. This principle underpins the work of City-REDI, the City-Region Economic Development Institute, at the University of Birmingham. It provides a real-world example of an attempt to improve the precision of policy interventions to improve regional economic growth pathways.

4.1 City-REDI

The UK's over-centralised government structure and a lack of devolved power and resources at the local level have reduced the 'quality' and capacity of institutions in regions outside of London and the greater South-East. Local agencies lack the resources, capacity and capability to intervene intelligently to improve their growth pathways. This means both analyse and deliver precise, targeted investments and interventions customised for the challenges and potential growth opportunities that their region offers.

This is the gap that City-REDI at the University of Birmingham was designed to fill, and examples of its work feature throughout this Element.[1] A key aim, driven by regional stakeholders as the main research users, has been to increase the precision of policy interventions, across a wide range of areas, from business support or skills and training programmes to public R&D investments. Helping policymakers select locally appropriate interventions, and evaluate the relative costs, benefits and trade-offs in terms of different kinds of growth outcomes (productivity, inclusivity and/or sustainability) supports the better use of scarce public funds.

In the UK context, the growing need to improve productivity (wealth-creation capacity) while reducing inequality (improving wealth distribution) and improving sustainability also presented a set of policy trade-offs and challenges that policymakers needed additional analysis and evaluation tools to resolve. The spatial geography of economic impacts provides a distinctive, overarching theme to the institute's work. With policy insights revealed by examining the dynamics of regional growth at multiple levels. This includes deep-dive case studies to assess the effects of public investments into start-up

---

[1] The City-Region Economic Development Institute (City-REDI) at the University of Birmingham was established in 2015 with initial funding from the University and further investment in 2019 for the WMREDI programme from Research England, part of UK Research and Innovation (UKRI, the main university research funding agency in the UK). It has thirty staff in an interdisciplinary team of academic researchers, data and policy analysts, working with a coalition of regional and national stakeholders. It was recently awarded £3.6 million from the UKRI to act as the Local Policy Innovation Partnership Hub for the UK, leading a national consortium. This will develop a programme of capacity-building activities and further analysis of the challenges places face and what works in place partnerships.

City-REDI's main aim has been to support policymakers in promoting inclusive and sustainable economic growth at the local level. To do this, it combines short-term data analysis and policy inputs with long-term research to develop a better understanding of city-regions as complex, integrated and unique economic, political and social systems. As such, it developed as a hybrid organisation designed to connect academic rigour and objectivity with applied, practical user-oriented outputs. There is also a thematic and partly disciplinary division of labour as the team has selectively prioritised specific components of growth, including skills, innovation, local institutions and governance structures across a variety of industry sectors, different sizes of firms and value chains, and socio-economic communities. Always with a focus on the spatial dimensions of cause and effect, which is novel compared to other policy institutions and think-tanks.

incubators, STEM assets or 'innovation intermediaries', for example (referenced in this Element). Industry sector surveys and comparative surveys on, for example, productivity constraints or business support programmes sit alongside the analysis of socio-economic change over time in households and communities.

4.1.1 REDI Toolkits

Within the portfolio of methodological approaches, there are a number of frameworks and tools, including logic chains, cost–benefit analysis, modelling, economic impact and multiplier effects. One example is the City-REDI multi-regional input–output (MRIO) model. This provides insights into the input–output relationships between industries at the regional level, and interregional trade spillovers to show the transmission of impacts from one region to another. The model has been applied, for example, to university student spending across UK regions to show significant regional variation in the resulting multiplier effects on GVA (and per capita GVA, a measure of productivity) and jobs created. London benefits the most from all spillover flows, because of the scale of its local economy and the number of firms based there. But Greater Manchester and the Birmingham city-region also benefit more from student spending, relative to other places because of the higher levels of absorptive capacity in these regions. That is, more firms involved in the value chains that supply the products and services that students spend their money on are local to these bigger city-regions (Carrascal Incera et al., 2022). As a focused example of the value of the model, the study shows how comparable patterns of spending create different local growth impacts depending on the industry structure of the region. More broadly, the MRIO model, alongside other evaluation tools, enables City-REDI analysts to estimate the multiplier effects of changes in spending or different kinds of new investments in a region, to that region. This then provides insights for policymakers wanting to understand the growth impacts of different kinds of government investments.

As background, it is worth noting that policymakers tend to assume that a £1 million public investment or subsidy into skills, transport infrastructure, science parks, R&D or amenities exclusively benefits the region receiving the investment. In fact, the interregional direct and indirect production and consumption multipliers are difficult to trace without modelling the relevant interregional effects. This complexity is often missing from policy analysis. It also helps us understand how, and to what degree, dominant cities like London, which host most firms (and headquarters), receive larger relative shares of the spillovers from consumption spending and investment in all regions.

4.1.2 When We Aim to Become Part of the Solution, We Often Reveal More of the Problem

The work of City-REDI outlined in this Section has undoubtedly made a positive difference to regional growth policy in the UK. But in the process, the scale and the entrenched, path-dependent nature of the problem has become clearer. The analysis of the local economic impacts of student spending patterns described in Section 4.1.1 provides a good example of this.

The accumulated experience of City-REDI researchers alongside a wide range of studies point to the need to take a systemic approach to understanding regional economic growth. These also show that changing the trajectory of city-regions that have persistently low productivity and high levels of inequality requires more resources and a very different level of intervention than has been tried in the past. No less, we would argue, than a reinvention of the capitalist system. Failure to intervene will leave left-behind communities with worsening levels of deprivation.

City-REDI has taken a systemic approach in a number of ways. As indicated, long-term and short-term, multilevel and multidisciplinary research is needed. But it is also valuable to assess the impacts of growth along a broader logic chain than is often attempted. This means connecting the drivers of economic growth not just with the outputs, such as improved productivity, greater GDP, higher firm-level profitability, more and/or higher-income jobs, and so on, but also with the outcomes, including increased household income, reduced social benefits dependency in deprived communities, greater economic resilience at the regional level, and so on. Similarly, the impacts of slow or no-growth in regions, which leads to an equal and opposite logic chain of negative outcomes, can be tracked and measured. When places fail to attract investment, firms or skilled workers, the cycle of decline can mean lower productivity, fewer or lower-income jobs, increased social benefits dependency, worsening health and welfare, higher crime and mental health problems.

Different interventions would probably be selected if the full, long-term costs of declining regions were fully understood, but academic research and policy analysts have tended to specialise on one or the other side of this cycle. The UK Treasury and government departments also tend to disconnect economic growth from socio-economic safety nets, in the same way as most governments.

Studying the 'economic epidemiology' or regional transmission effects of the COVID pandemic to the West Midlands region, alongside other economic shocks (Brexit, the Ukraine war), helped reveal these kinds of dynamic connections. City-REDI studies have shown that the region, and others like it, have higher levels of exposure and lower levels of resilience, in the face of such shocks (Billing et al., 2019; Kitsos et al., 2023; Qamar et al., 2022). For example, Qamar et al. (2022) show how the West Midlands' economy is highly dependent, perhaps over-dependent, on the automotive manufacturing sector. Another study charts the knock-on effects of insolvencies, particularly among low-productivity, low-skilled small- and medium-sized enterprises (SMEs), to low-income communities and household deprivation levels (Collinson et al., 2023b). These estimate the wider socio-economic impacts of firm failure and increased unemployment, on local communities, that result from such shocks in the absence of specific kinds of intervention. But they also provide insights into what kinds of 'defensive' policies provide the best safety nets in difficult times, and which proactive policies can help overcome the barriers to growth in periods of opportunity.

The team at City-REDI shares a collective belief that more intelligent and targeted policy interventions can make a difference. The irony is that beliefs increasingly appear to be as important or possibly more important than data and empirical evidence as a foundation for driving large-scale change, for better or for worse. Some groups of people seem to be entrenched in beliefs that have no empirical basis and have little or no trust in those producing the evidence. This also needs changing.

For those without a strong belief in the current system of capitalism, we might be preaching to the converted when we call for change. But complete alternatives to market capitalism are very rare. For those with some belief in the capitalist systems of different varieties that dominate in every economy on the planet, we hope that the evidence above goes some way to convincing you that a major reinvention is needed.

5 Recommendations for New Varieties of Capitalism

Alternatives to capitalism are rare, but different varieties of capitalism thrive. However, the evidence summarised in Sections 2 and 3 tells us that a major reinvention is needed to make advanced economies like the UK fit for purpose in a changing world. Incremental changes to current structures are unlikely to bring about the level of change in the timeframe needed. Further evidence on why change is now imperative comes from studies that show a persistent relationship between inequality, slower economic growth, weaker social cohesion and political instability (Eatwell and Goodwin, 2018; Piketty, 2020; Rodríguez-Pose, 2018).

This is not just about spending public funding more effectively and efficiently. It is also more than a moral imperative to reduce inequality. Failure to address these serious socio-economic imbalances will fuel further discontent, which could be increasingly voiced outside of the current channels for challenging the political and economic elites. It will also contribute to a longer-term decline in economic efficiency and therefore living standards. Finally, it will reduce the chances that the kinds of decisive, stable and trusted governance that is needed to tackle climate change will be established in the timescale required.

A fundamental shift to government structures that proactively enable, rather than simply react, monitor and control, is required to support the implementation of these recommendations. The institutions, governance mechanisms and wider political arena that underpin the selection mechanisms for directing resource allocation and moderating wealth distribution need to change. But enabling more distributed growth clusters will be more viable in the long run than providing an increasingly expensive safety net to limit the damaging effects of socio-economic inequalities.

Enabling inclusive growth means creating the conditions for higher levels of wealth creation in regions outside of London and the South-East of England. It also means policy interventions to promote a more even distribution of the benefits of wealth creation, including from national public investments. In the following, we first outline the kind of policy regime that could make a difference to uneven growth patterns in the UK context. If the evidence presented in the previous sections answer the question of 'why' change is needed, this is the 'how'. Then we examine the need for local industry strategies as the focus of policy interventions (the 'what'). These two elements are combined in a final section on RIS. Stronger RIS would support productivity and economic growth at the local level and particular kinds of innovation would enable more inclusivity.

5.1 The Policy Regime

Our key recommendation, first and foremost, is for more devolved resources, decision-making power and accountability at the local level. One of the reasons this Element, and the work of City-REDI, focuses on regional economic systems and geographic disparities is because the over-centralised governance structure of the UK is at the heart of the problems we have identified. The spatial concentration of investment and the local capacity to create wealth and to benefit from this wealth mirror the concentration of public resource allocation, political power and the capacity to deliver change. The embedded structural bias towards already thriving local economies needs to be reversed (Coyle and Sensier, 2020; Green, 2023).

Studies indicate that neither extreme fiscal decentralisation nor extreme fiscal centralisation are particularly good for economic growth. There is strong evidence that the UK, termed 'hyper-centralised' relative to OECD counterparts, is too centralised and would benefit from greater sub-national fiscal decentralisation. Greater sub-national decentralisation is also associated with higher levels of interregional convergence with fewer geographic economic inequalities (Ezcurra and Rodríguez-Pose, 2013). Moreover, tax decentralisation does correlate with improved regional productivity (Blöchliger and Akgun, 2018). So further devolution is very likely to support faster, more distributed growth and reduce inequality. Decentralisation, and better alignment between local revenue-generation and expenditure, would also generate greater returns to public investments, partly because local economic development policies would be designed for local conditions (Bailey et al., 2023; Stansbury et al., 2023).

The successful implementation of devolved growth policies in turn requires strong coalitions of public- and private-sector stakeholders (Flanagan et al., 2023; Tilley et al., 2023). Greater devolution of resources incentivises local partnerships to reach a consensus on the kinds of interventions needed and to support successful delivery of growth plans.

The second proposition, in terms of alleviating challenges that undermine the wider policy regime, is for policies that are much better connected across thematic areas, instead of siloed, in distinctive (often competing) ministerial departments (business and trade, education, transport, health, energy, science, innovation and technology etc.). A coordinated, system-wide set of interventions in transport, housing, education and skills, business support and innovation (and other factor endowments), at the national and local levels is needed to underpin targeted interventions for inclusive growth (Bailey et al., 2019).

Better coordination between and across the various dimensions of policy, to support more problem-oriented regional industrial policies, has been proposed by a number of studies (Flanagan et al., 2023). There is also a consensus that changes in the structure and the quality of the relevant institutions is a necessary prerequisite (Rodríguez-Pose, 2020) for long-term, locally appropriate and coherent infrastructure and skills development. This relates to both the call for more devolved capacity and capability in regions, and to the need to focus on improving RIS (Belso-Martinez et al., 2024), which we focus on in Section 5.4.

Third, such interventions need to be precise and customised to local conditions. It is not controversial to argue for more sophisticated, precise and adaptive policy interventions, which are customised to the challenges and growth potential of different sub-national regions. But in practice it is challenging to balance long-term, stable development policies for regional growth, with quicker, more responsive and locally led initiatives to improve resilience in the face of economic shocks and support a transition into new growth areas. The former would support more comprehensive and predictable programmes of investment in education and infrastructure, for example, and provide more certainty to private investors. The latter would help regional economies customise market interventions to suit their distinctive growth challenges and opportunities (Tilley et al., 2023). Balancing these objectives calls for some degree of policy 'ambidexterity'.

Tying these together, decentralisation in the UK case is likely to enable government to be more responsive to local needs, for example, in education or infrastructure (Bianchi, Giorcelli, and Martino, 2023). It is also likely to help government leverage local knowledge and coordination externalities through the delivery of simultaneous interventions in infrastructure, skills and other policy domains (Rodrik, 2000; Rodrik and Sabel, 2019).

The 'binding constraints' identified by analysis outlined in Section 3.1 and informed by the challenges of development traps provide a useful list of priority areas, but the specifics will vary by place. Precise means appropriate prioritisation and targeting of place-specific constraints, beyond the generic. For example, within skills development programmes, there is a need to focus on the types of skills most in demand by local firms and most likely to enhance productivity. Business support programmes, from those designed to reduce insolvencies and reduce unemployment to those aimed at scaling up local small firms, should select firms with the greatest local multiplier effects as well as the potential to grow. Selecting the wrong skills or the wrong firms wastes scarce public resources. Policy interventions like these should also be more robustly evaluated, linked to broader regional growth plans, and targets adjusted for continuous improvement. There is evidence to show that much of this does not happen and there is a gap between high-level political narratives and policy ambitions, and on-the-ground implementation (Collinson et al., 2023a; Newman et al., 2023). This takes us back to the lack of devolved capacity and capability to deliver more targeted interventions.

More specific inclusive growth initiatives, such as the commuter's credit for lower-skilled, lower-income households, or an equivalent to the Earned Income Tax Credit in the United States, for example, should be customised to target particular occupational groups and/or communities with the greatest potential to impact overall regional growth. Over the long term, the combination of policy interventions should help regions break out of 'development traps' characterised by a dominance of legacy, declining industry sectors and accelerating the transition to new growth sectors. Improving RIS is critical to achieving this transition and supporting more adaptive and resilient, as well as sustainable and inclusive, regional economies.

5.2 Maximising the Impact of Business Support

The point made about precision interventions targeting the right kinds of firms is worth developing further here. There is a gap between the aspirations and principles of economic (and inclusive) growth policies and on-the-ground delivery of these policies. Closing this gap by improving the mechanisms applied to select which firms are supported with scarce public funding could potentially make a significant difference to local growth (Collinson, 2022). This in turn requires local capability to deliver precise policy interventions.

At the most basic level, funding for local business support tends to fall into one of three areas. (1) Public investments in entrepreneurial start-ups, (2) growth (or scale-up) subsidies for SMEs, and (3) 'safety net' support to limit the number of insolvencies (and reduce unemployment), again mainly for SMEs. The Coronavirus Business Interruption Loan Scheme and furlough payments to reduce unemployment during the COVID pandemic in the UK are examples of the latter, and these were available to all firms. Outside of a major economic shock, only a limited number of firms can be helped and, in simple terms, investing in local firms that are unlikely to grow or create jobs or improve productivity is a waste of public resources. However, this has been found to be a common practice (Hart, 2023). Delivery of such schemes is often devolved to Combined Authorities or local councils, and in the past, LEPs (Local Enterprise Partnerships) until they were 'decommissioned', where there is often a lack of capability and capacity to identify and co-opt firms with the most potential to add value, is a recognised problem (Bramley et al., 2021).

Additional precision in the business support selection process would enable limited amounts of public resources to be better targeted at firms that (1) would trigger significant future costs if they went into insolvency, from unemployment benefits, household welfare payments, healthcare and crime prevention (Lyons, Ma and Collinson, 2025), and/or (2) had the greatest growth potential, and (3) the most significant local multiplier effects if they prospered over the long term. In all such policy initiatives, calculating the regional 'embeddedness' of these firms is key to understanding their economic importance to the local economy and whether they are 'worth' supporting (Collinson, 2022).

Embeddedness partly relates to 'stickiness' or the likelihood that a firm (or one of its functional divisions) will stay or leave a place. Fixed assets, for example, tend to increase embeddedness, which is why regional authorities like to target manufacturing firms as preferred inward investors. But embeddedness also relates to the spatial configuration of the value chains and supply chains within which a firm operates. These in turn create local multipliers that can be measured in terms of investment, employment and productivity as contributors to the local economy. Multipliers are both upstream and downstream, taking into account both the demand-pull effects of a firm buying from another local firms, and the impacts of its employees (and those of its suppliers) as consumers spending on local goods and services.

This has been analysed at City-REDI by taking the average of three ratios, the percentage of regional to non-regional suppliers, sales and employees. The higher the average, the greater the proportion of suppliers, sales and/or employees that are local, rather than non-local, and this indicates a higher level of embeddedness. This in turn means that the region is relatively more dependent on this firm and its multipliers as a contributor to the local economy. It also means that the firm is more dependent on the region, so if suppliers become more expensive, the pool of skilled employees declines, or if customers leave the region, this kind of highly embedded firm will struggle more, with a greater likelihood of insolvency than less embedded firms (Billing et al., 2020).

The connection with inclusive growth is important and relates to the co-dependence between firms and households. When a supplier employs low-income workers on the basis of a contract with a local buyer, this can be the only flow of income preventing a low-income household slipping into benefits dependency and poverty. Supporting more embedded firms or industry sectors during economic shocks is an important target for local policymakers. Limiting insolvencies across this group of firms is important for inclusivity, because the poorest households are hit hardest when economic shocks increase the bankruptcy rate, partly because less competitive SMEs with low-skilled, low-wage employees tend to be the first to fall (Collinson et al., 2023b; Lyons, Ma and Collinson, 2025). Most of the time, however, public funding is allocated without any consideration of these differences.

At another level of aggregation, local industrial embeddedness is defined as the 'share of regional interindustry economic activity that is anchored to a region' and is a focus of research on smart specialisation and regional economic resilience (Kitsos et al., 2023). Assessing the relative embeddedness of legacy industries or the potential benefits of investing in emergent industries for the regional economy is an important component of a sensible industrial strategy. Interventions to provide safety nets when economic shocks threaten to deepen development traps, as in the case of the West Midlands (UK) automotive manufacturing sector (Qamar et al., 2022), is one dimension of this. Another is the need to focus on growth sectors that a region may have 'latent' competitive advantages to underpin future growth. For example, the East Midlands (UK) region has the potential for developing a local upstream space sector (spacecraft, launch equipment, satellites), given a combination of skills, manufacturing assets, alignment with specialist science, technology and expertise in local universities. But these assets and capabilities are not easy to identify in combination, and there is a question mark about the region's 'legitimacy' as a leader in emergent technologies underlying this sector, which limits public funding to leverage its potential (Billing et al., 2024).

Finally, selecting the 'right kinds of firms' to target for support can be seen as a central pillar for a variety of intended outcomes, including and beyond inclusivity. With better data on local firms, public resources could be targeted at firms that are committed to upskilling, enabling lower-income employees, or the unemployed to improve their household income (reducing inequality). But firms that invest relatively higher amounts into sustainable business practices, recycling or achieving net-zero CO_2 emissions could also (or alternatively) be privileged if the aim was to accelerate progress towards UNSDG, the seventeen UN Sustainable Development Goals.

5.3 Leveraging Public Procurement

Although public resources for business support is limited in many countries, national spending through public procurement channels is significant. It has also increased as a share of GDP in the past ten years across the OECD, from 11.8% of GDP in 2007 to 12.9% of GDP in 2021, and 14.8% across OECD–EU countries. In the UK, it has also increased from 13.1% (2019) to 15.7% (2021), and gross spending on public-sector procurement was £393 billion in 2022–2023 across the UK (OECD, 2023b). Spending the same amount in different ways, to achieve some of the outcomes outlined here through the targeting of locally embedded firms, provides an opportunity to accelerate and shape local development pathways.

A City-REDI pilot study with the Centre for Local Economic Strategies (CLES) and eight 'anchor institutions' in the Birmingham city-region with a combined budget of around £4 billion and a workforce of over 40,000 provided some insights into the potential. This estimated that if all eight were to increase procurement spend with Birmingham-based businesses by 1.8% per year, this would add £23.4 million per year to the city economy and create nearly 800 new jobs (CLES, 2018; Parke, 2021). Rather than increasing spending, the project identified opportunities to switch from non-local suppliers to firms embedded in the region, without increased costs or any compromise to quality or delivery. Targeting this additional spend and a larger proportion of the remaining 98.2% of spending in the ways we have discussed here could have significant impacts on inclusive regional growth.

A more sophisticated use of public procurement, which links us to the discussion about RIS in Section 5.4, is innovation-orientated public procurement. This can create 'lead customers' or 'lead markets' for innovative products, services, or processes, or act as an incentive for developers of new technologies, in parallel with existing R&D funding subsidies (Bento et al., 2022; Uyarra et al., 2020). This involves changes in supplier selection mechanisms and to government procurement contracts to build in specific innovation-related goals, which relate to wider development targets. It is particularly being seen as a way of accelerating the development, adoption and diffusion of sustainable technologies to support net-zero goals as it can stimulate both the 'demand pull' and 'supply push' side of innovation pipelines.

Mazzucato (2020) uses public procurement as an illustration of how the state should be seen as a co-creator of value, rather than being limited in both economic theory and policy studies to 'fixing markets' and 'enabling' or de-risking the private sector. Governments regularly enable value creation and redistribute value by investing and taking risks to co-shape markets with the private sector. A deeper understanding of this role and public–private relationships and public options in investment decision-making (rather than performance defined by dividend yields or GVA per capita) would ensure that more 'public investment delivers for the public interest'.

There are a range of challenges to any ambition to leverage public procurement in these ways in countries around the world. To begin with, government departments would need to move away from a focus on short-term cost-savings and have faith in longer-term planning targets. Changes in procurement practices, based on research and intelligence about the likely impacts of different kinds of approaches in different places, alongside regulatory changes, improved skills and more capacity at the local level, would also be needed.

The UK arguably has additional constraints, linked to the policy regime already described. First of all, public procurement is highly centralised in the UK relative to EU and OECD comparators and has become more centralised over the past decade. The 2015 data shows UK as the only large EU economy with highly centralised procurement spending at 63% of the total compared to France at just over 30% and Germany at 15%. The 2021 data suggests that it has become more centralised with almost 75% of public procurement decisions made by central government departments (OECD, 2023b).

One of the benefits of leaving Brexit was expected to be a release from EU procurement regulation to enable better use of procurement as a policy tool. But there has been a significant additional burden on the UK civil service and government legal departments from the need to unravel long-standing procurement rules and create a new set. At the same time, there are clear signs that a lack of capacity and capability in government procurement departments at the local level provides a significant advantage for private-sector contractors and a stronger focus on short-term yields at the expense of long-term policy objectives.

5.4 Strengthening Regional Innovation Systems

The state plays an important role in promoting and distributing the benefits of innovation, from R&D tax subsidies for firms and schemes to attract FDI in R&D, to the direct funding of public R&D that crowds-in private investment. It also has a strong influence on the higher education sector where much of the funding goes to stimulate innovation, as discussed. Connecting FE and HE to local skills needs as part of a wider industrial strategy should also be a priority. This in turn should link up with housing and transport planning. But the key focus is to improve RIS in a way that distributes the benefits locally, reducing inequalities rather than just raising GVA per head or productivity (Collinson, 2024a; Kitagawa, 2024).

Other varieties of capitalism already support stronger RIS that both create wealth and deliver the benefits more widely. Recent analysis by Lee (2024) draws on case studies of Taiwan, Sweden, Austria, and Switzerland, which combine highly innovative economies with higher-than-average levels of equality (low Gini coefficients). These countries provide insights into how the government can intervene to make innovation and shared prosperity mutually reinforcing. Taylor (2022) also provides some insights from international comparisons drawing on the experience of the UK's short-lived Industrial Strategy Council.

An initial scoping study at City-REDI compared UK and European RIS by differentiating R&D inputs from outputs using a principal components analysis to produce separate indices (Ioramashvili et al., 2022b). It shows that some regions are good at basic research and the development of new technologies, and others are good at the commercialisation of these inputs to produce new or improved processes, products or services. Few regions appear to be good at both. The UK performs relatively well in terms of innovation inputs across most regions, but apart from the South-East, and the East of England, it is lagging international counterparts in terms of applying these commercially.

The analysis compared 237 European regions and found that many regions in Germany and some in the North of Italy face the same challenge, despite being successful at engineering and manufacturing. Some regions, particularly in Norway and France, appear to have the opposite problem, with weak basic research and relative strengths in the commercialisation of new technologies. Only Belgium and the Netherlands perform relatively well both in terms of innovation inputs and outputs. These countries appear to have a better balance between the supply-side of innovation inputs and the demand-side of outputs and adoption.

Alongside its potential to perform better overall, the UK appears to have a 'two-speed' innovation economy, mirroring the spatial divides described in Sections 2 and 3. This is why it should develop a much stronger set of differentiated, locally focused RIS policies. While Nafizah and Roper (2024) also support this view, they provide insights into what local policies should target in different regions, drawing a slightly different spatial divide. Their study reveals four 'baseline' regions (Scotland, North-East, Yorks and Humber, East of England) where firms are performing as expected, in that their propensity for innovation is consistent with the enablers and barriers experienced locally. Support in these regions should focus on helping firms become more innovative, reducing the barriers and boosting the enablers. This contrasts a group of 'over-performing' regions (including the North-West, East Midlands, West Midlands, London, South-East, South-West) where local firms appear to be much better at 'translating the enablers into higher innovation propensity', that is, their propensity for innovation is significantly greater than that which would be expected, given the local enablers (Nafizah and Roper, 2024). In these places, the focus should be on generating more value from innovation. Different kinds of financing, such as R&D tax credits, innovation grants and intellectual property support, plus expert advice on business process, planning and development or product/service development, support for particular kinds of skills are among the enablers. But these vary in their importance by region, in parallel to the relevant barriers, and this needs to be the basis for localised policy interventions.

5.4.1 Universities as Drivers of Improved RIS

Given the calibre of UK universities, there is significant scope to improve the capacity and capability at the regional level to translate university-based R&D into new or improved processes, products and services. As outlined earlier in this Element, HE institutions fund 8% (£5.6 billion) but perform 25% (£14.9 billion) of UK R&D (Panjwani, 2023). They also have a strong economic impact, as shown in reports produced by London Economics, which suggest that as much as half of the total economic contribution of a university can be attributed to the 'impact of research and knowledge exchange'. In 2021/2022, research and related commercialisation activities for the twenty-four research-intensive Russell Group of universities added £37.6 billion to the UK economy and supported more than 250,000 jobs (London Economics, 2024). The analysis estimates that for every £1 of public funds invested in

Russell Group research at these institutions, more than £8.50 was generated for the UK economy. For Oxford University, for example, this amounts to £7.9 billion (and 28,000 jobs) out of a total impact of £15.7 billion. This is a significant amount and consists of 'research activities' (29%) and 'knowledge exchange activities' (22%). This is more than the impact generated by university procurement (£6 billion) and far larger than teaching and learning activities, 'educational exports', and the University's contribution to tourism combined (London Economics, 2021).

Universities feature strongly in the stylised framing of an RIS, shown in Figure 1. But the long-running consensus is that the UK still suffers from a more challenging 'valley of death' than most countries, limiting the commercialisation of university-based R&D. This means that there is the significant potential to increase the rate of R&D commercialisation and, critically, to support local value appropriation to boost RIS in regions that need it the most (Bailey et al., 2018). Two areas of focus are important; university spinouts, and innovation intermediaries that combine technology transfer, knowledge exchange and upskilling.

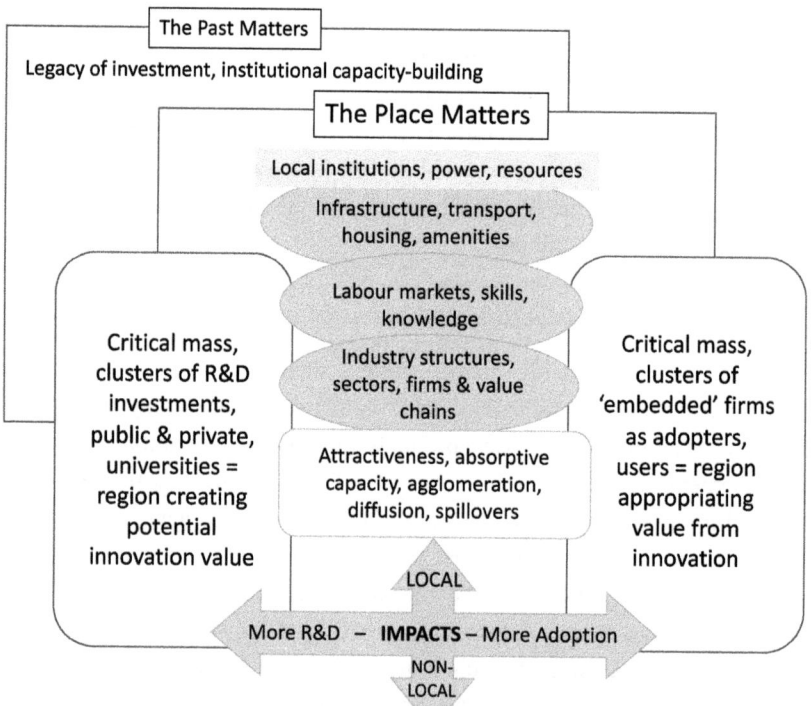

Figure 1 Regional innovation systems: place matters. Adapted from Collinson et al. (2024b)

5.4.2 Spinouts and Start-Ups

In terms of UK spinouts, recent evidence pushes back on the myth that UK universities are less active in producing these than their US counterparts (Ulrichsen and Roupakia, 2024). In fact, when we take into the much larger size and number of US universities, the two countries are fairly similar in terms of the number of spinouts produced. University spinouts in the UK make up a large percentage of top-ranking start-ups in terms of investment (60% of the top twenty-five pharmaceutical and biotech start-ups, 44% of healthcare devices start-ups, and 28% of semiconductor start-ups) (Ulrichsen and Roupakia, 2024). Moreover, key to our focus, universities outside London and the South-East of England generate similar numbers of spinouts per £100 million of research income as their larger counterparts inside this region, but receive less public R&D investment. Smaller research universities in London and the South-East of England actually produce fewer spinouts per £100million than their counterparts in other UK regions (Ulrichsen and Roupakia, 2024).

As acknowledged, rebalancing public investment by increasing funding to support spinouts from universities in lagging regions is a priority. But a related challenge is to reduce the incidence of relocation (often linked to buy-outs), and to provide incentives to embed successful start-ups into their place of origin, so that they trigger local employment multipliers, value appropriation and longer-term clustering in the region. Spinouts alone very often do not have strong regional growth impacts. A significant proportion of the firms that account for the data summarised here, which boost the numbers for Oxford and in even more so for Cambridge (almost twice as much according to London Economics, 2023), are in this category. Firms like Oxford Nanopore Technologies and Cambridge Epigenetix (renamed Biomodal) have very high financial valuations after rounds of venture capital investment and do have the potential to become global high-tech firms. But if and when they scale up, there is often limited local employment or multiplier effects through local supply chains in the local region. Moreover, in places like Cambridge and to a certain extent Oxford, there are much smaller industrial hinterlands than universities in city-regions like Birmingham and Manchester. There is arguably more local value appropriation from the higher volume of small-scale technology transfer and knowledge exchange activities in these city-regions, although this has yet to be measured robustly.

5.4.3 STEM Assets

This leads to the second area of focus, 'STEM assets', defined as 'physical facilities' dedicated largely to the 'translation, development and transfer of scientific, technological or engineering innovation and knowledge and expertise which relates to new or improved business processes, products or services' (Billing et al., 2023). Evidence suggests certain kinds of STEM assets are embedded locally, linking university R&D and skills and knowledge to local firms, and often to SMEs. This is particularly important when the latter form part of the productivity tail, which is the case in UK city-regions in the Midlands and the North, particularly associated with manufacturing supply chains. In such contexts, the impacts of, for example, the Manufacturing Technology Centre and Warwick Manufacturing Group are significant (Ioramashvili et al., 2022a). There is evidence that they improve the competitiveness of local SMEs and therefore support a more inclusive form of economic growth, because upskilling workers in these firms increases income flows into lower-income communities. Contrast this with strategies to attract R&D-intensive functions to city-regions, which can displace low-income workers by attracting larger numbers of higher-paid R&D workers (Ciarli et al., 2018) and inflating local prices. This is one example of the complex trade-offs between inclusivity and productivity in policy decision-making.

Overall, STEM assets are an essential and underinvested component of strong RIS infrastructures in the UK, partly because they combine upskilling with technology transfer to improve local innovative capabilities (Billing et al., 2023; Ioramashvili et al., 2022a; Jibril et al., 2024). They can also potentially accelerate the transition from legacy industry sectors to emergent, higher-growth industries (Collinson, 2023). Initial analyses suggest that there are nascent or latent advantages in large city-regions, particularly observable when we look beyond standard industrial classifications (SIC codes). Real-time industrial classifications, for example, have been used recently by the UK government to understand more about these hidden advantages to support investment into regional clusters (DSIT, 2024). By working with local firms in legacy industries and particularly with SMEs in manufacturing supply chains where productivity is low, STEM assets support the diffusion of technologies, processes and practices (through skills development) that can improve productivity in existing industry sectors and/or help firms move into new business sectors.

This certainly points to the significant potential in the commercialisation of a larger proportion of university-based R&D, better leveraged to improve local firm-level productivity as well as strengthening the RIS in the hinterlands of research-intensive universities. This would also increase spillovers ('unpriced and unintentional knowledge externalities') that have been shown to support local economic growth, despite the difficulties in measuring how much (Becker et al., 2023). Advocates of 'pro-productivity policies' similarly point to the need for more investment in the diffusion of better innovation practices in these regions (van Ark et al., 2024).

5.4.4 Customising Interventions: The Past and the Place Matter

Figure 1 provides a high-level framework that aims to capture the various features and flows of a generic RIS. When developing policy interventions for stronger RIS, the key point is that R&D inputs, such as investments in university science and technology, spinouts, or science parks, do not necessarily boost local growth. More specifically, there is significant variation in the type of growth and the rate of growth, which results from different combinations of inputs. The past matters because long-term investments in the main endowments listed make a difference to a region's propensity to generate and leverage innovation for local growth. The place matters because each region has a unique combination of endowments, different challenges and different potential, in terms of future growth pathways. So, different combinations of interventions are needed in different places.

On the one side of this framework (Figure 1), we might have a critical mass and/or specialised cluster of R&D investments, public and private universities, R&D-intensive firms and advanced skills representing a set of inputs with the potential for adding value locally. Patents are good indicators of this supply-side capacity (Cambridge produces a lot of them) but are often used as proxy measures of innovation, or even the strength of a regional economy, which is misleading. Estimates suggest that less than 15% of all patents are commercialised. Appropriating value from invention requires other factors to be present. Moreover, additional conditions have to be in place for the commercialisation process to benefit the local economy.

On the other side of the framework, a critical mass or specialised clusters of firms as adopters and users of innovation enables a region to appropriate value from innovation inputs. A long-term EU policy initiative has explored how different combinations of firms underpin different kinds of regional growth and resilience and require a variety of interventions. Much of the focus has been on the benefits and trade-offs that result from forms of 'smart specialisation' (Balland et al., 2019, 2022; Iammarino et al., 2019; Pinheiro et al., 2022). The benefits of better alignment between the supply and demand sides of this framework have been explored less, from a more general region-wide perspective. But there has been analysis, for example, on how strong partnerships between co-located firms and universities can increase knowledge transfer and the exploitation of 'invention for innovation' to boost local economic growth.

The 'moderators' of this relationship, listed in the centre of Figure 1, are the other components of a region that underpin its attractiveness, for investors, firms and skilled workers. The quality of local institutions and infrastructure, the presence of high-level and/or specialist labour, clusters of innovative firms and related value chains are all important. The presence of these, alongside stronger absorptive capacity, mechanisms that support diffusion and/or spillovers, and a tendency towards specialist agglomerations, all help underpin a stronger RIS. As we have discussed in Section 5.2, when firms are more embedded and linked to local value chains, more of the impacts and benefits from the appropriation of value from innovation stay in the region.

Policy interventions should be coordinated across all of these areas. A clear starting point for the UK is to redress the spatial imbalance in government R&D funding outlined in Section 2.3. One analysis of this 'supply-side bias' looks at the additional public R&D funding that would be channelled into the West Midlands region under different rebalancing scenarios. If the UK government invested equally in every UK region, the West Midlands would receive an additional £0.91 billion. If it matched private R&D spending in UK regions, the West Midlands would get an additional £1.06 billion (Forth and Jones, 2020). Intelligently targeted in the ways we have discussed, this would make a significant difference over time.

We have discussed the need for high-quality institutions at the regional level and more devolved resources elsewhere in this Element. Below this category in Figure 1, we have infrastructure, transport, housing and amenities, all of which are important for attracting skilled workers and firms to a place. Access to skills is a major constraint on innovation and growth for businesses. At the same time, access to employment and pathways to high-income employment are key for inclusivity. Developments in transport infrastructure that are designed to bridge the gap between the demand and supply of particular types of skills in regions should focus on linking firms with specific types of skill needs, with residential housing priced at the appropriate income levels. This can include physical infrastructure, including roads, bus lanes or public railways. But it can also focus on travel subsidies to help improve the efficiency of local labour markets. These connect both sides of the inclusive growth coin, helping firms improve competitiveness and helping households improve income and resilience. The next section examines how we can ensure that the benefits from improved growth are more widely distributed than in the past.

5.5 Developing Inclusive Regional Innovation Systems

Neil Lee's recent book *Innovation for the Masses* points to US examples of local inequalities, including the San Francisco Bay Area, which is home to the millionaire founders of high-tech start-ups and a large number of homeless people with no assets or income. The top 1% of households have forty-eight times more wealth than the bottom 50%. He suggests that this is a global problem; where top-class universities and high-tech firms cluster, there are high levels of inequality because value created in these strong RIS is appropriated by small elites (Lee, 2024).

The UK government and others around the world quite often focus on high-tech, R&D-led growth policies, with the assumption that most regions have the potential to be the next silicon-something (valley, glen, fen etc.). They don't. But the more important point is that this kind of growth, including investment in spinouts and R&D-intensive firms, tends not to create extensive multiplier effects that benefit the wider economy. As noted by Lee (2024), if successful, these approaches increase the proportion of technology-intensive firms (locally grown and from inward investment) and support better-skilled, higher-income workers. However, this affects a relatively small number of firms, jobs and economic activity in a region (Hansen, 2022) and it can also displace low-skilled workers through higher local housing costs and increase unemployment (Ciarli et al., 2018). Cambridge is an interesting example, with higher productivity, but significant inequality, similar to the San Francisco Bay Area.

On the other side of the policy coin, a second approach is to focus on increasing levels of employment among low-skilled, low-income groups to limit unemployment. Clearly necessary, during economic shocks, but arguably in the UK, this has the effect of subsidising low-skilled labour, rather than upskilling or investing in capital to improve productivity. Data summarised in Section 3.1 shows that UK firms invest less than their counterparts in other advanced economies in both skills and capital. The most automated countries in the world are South Korea, Singapore, Japan, Germany, and Sweden, with notably high levels of robotics and productivity. The UK is a laggard in this respect and some policies are delaying a much-needed industrial transition in many sectors away from a reliance on cheaper, less-skilled labour, which is part of the inequality problem.

This takes us back to the challenge of managing policy trade-offs between productivity and inclusivity. Innovation provides some of the means by which wealth creation and more inclusive systems of wealth distribution can work together. STEM assets, and a range of similar interventions, can stimulate several different types of development pathways, including a balanced, inclusive approach. This would focus on upskilling and improved absorptive capacity in local firms, particularly process innovation in local SMEs. It strikes at the heart of the UK low-productivity tail and enables access to new skills and higher incomes for low-income workers. These schemes improve plant-level efficiency, service delivery or product or service quality and can also drive up exports, an indicator of improved competitiveness. As described in Section 5.3, innovation procurement policies that set targets for government procurement to privilege local small firms in contracting mechanisms also has the potential to support more inclusive RIS (Uyarra et al., 2020).

More widely, strengthening the RIS in such regions should encompass demand-led innovation in the 'foundational economy' (FE) and public-sector service delivery (Morgan, 2019). The FE has received attention as a policy focus across Europe in recent years (Martynovich et al., 2023). This is the part of the local economy that 'creates and distributes goods and services consumed by all', at every level of income and social status, including 'material infrastructures' such as utilities and transportation, and 'providential services' including health and education. Innovation and longer-term investment in skills and processes would make these more efficient, benefitting all, rather than a smaller elite.

What this suggests is that linking innovation with better distributional outcomes is not solely about interventions that distribute the outputs and wealth created from innovation more evenly. It means directly involving a wider range of socio-economic groups and firms, through upskilling and other investments, in the innovation capacity-building process itself, across key sectors of the local economy. These are part of the solution, when the policy regime focuses on enabling growth and wealth creation alongside wealth distribution. This theme is continued in the conclusions in the following, final Section.

6 Conclusions

Recent commentary on the UK situation as a 'failing state' (Dorling, 2023) and the wider 'crisis of democratic capitalism' globally (Wolf, 2023) highlight a serious concern that democracy will be discarded as a key contributor to increasing inequality. Recent developments in the United States have further complicated and disrupted the global geopolitical situation, reducing the prospects of positive change.

The varieties of capitalism that have evolved in the UK and the United States are serving a wealthy sub-set of the population and leaving behind the rest. In some quarters, the wealthy are seen as having appropriated the democratic system to maintain this bias. This reminds us of how advanced civilisations have ended historically when the spiral of economic decline, political self-interest and social deprivation has reached a tipping point. But most would argue (particularly in the absence of radical alternatives that have ever worked) that basic capitalism does work when the institutional and governance mechanisms for funding, taxation, control and regulation are efficient, effective and fair.

So, at the broadest level, there is a need to get 'back to basics' in terms of how these capitalist systems operate. This includes clear incentives for people to earn, save and invest alongside mechanisms for allocating resources efficiently and effectively, to propositions that add value. Added value includes profits that can be reinvested and surplus income for driving consumption. Arguably, one of the mechanisms that appears to be failing is the City, or financial services sector, which has the role of allocating resources for (long term) value creation. The other is the policy regime, which is increasingly preoccupied with short-term budgeting, rather than long-term investment (in infrastructure and education, for example) and driven more by political choreography and perception than targeted interventions or a commitment to real change. Both have evolved in the UK away from their fundamental roles in a capitalist system. But the challenge is bigger and more complex than this.

Gordon Redding in this CUP Elements Series (Redding, 2023) frames societal progress, across different varieties of capitalism, as contingent on the integrated workings of three sets of processes. These are an 'inspiring context', a 'transformative capacity' and 'empowered action'. The 'political role is that of balancing the influences across the total'. Fundamental change is arguably needed across all of these dimensions. This Element has had to take a narrower focus, but the aim has been to connect these macro-level grand challenges with micro-level insights and practical recommendations for improved policy interventions. This is one, perhaps essential, step in a wider reinvention of capitalism.

We began with a simple logic chain of cyclical stagnation in specific UK regions, measured in terms of their capacity to create wealth and the standards of living enjoyed by the local population. A series of indicators provide clear signs of the failure of the current variety of capitalism, with the UK as the lead example. Data on productivity (GVA per capita), transport infrastructure, education and skills, the distribution of income, assets and wealth, relative poverty, social mobility and health all show high levels of underinvestment and a notable overall slowdown in growth. They also show a significant spatial polarisation in regional capacity to create wealth outside of London and the greater South-East of England. This is matched by a growing polarisation between those with higher incomes, bigger assets, more life opportunities and better health outcomes, and the rest, left behind.

Understanding this challenge and how to rebalance the economy requires a systemic perspective combining different levels of analysis. The economics of uneven growth, which, for example, helps identify that the inadequate diffusion of productivity-enhancing practices between firms and places is one of the many causal factors, is one component. But economic factors are intimately tied up with the forms of institutional, financial and governance structures that determine, for example, the targeting of business support programmes. In combination, these underpin path dependencies that have helped concentrate stronger economic endowments in particular places and wealth in particular groups. Reversing the embedded structural bias that benefits already thriving local economies requires interventions that encompass political and policy-making regimes as well as an understanding of the economic dynamics at work.

With political power and public resources concentrated in London, the UK has about the most centralised governance structure among the OECD economies in terms of tax raising and spending powers. We recommend a fundamental change towards more devolved power over policy and resource-allocation decisions at the local level. An early priority should be to build capability and capacity in regional governance institutions at the heart of local coalitions to enable customised policy interventions. These should co-opt businesses, universities and other anchor institutions and connect across transport infrastructures, education and skills, business support, innovation and other areas relevant to economic growth. They should be precisely designed and delivered to focus on the best potential pathways, specific to each region, targeting the 'binding constraints' outlined in this Element. Escaping the entrenched path dependency and 'development traps' discussed in Section 3.1 also requires a certain degree of 'ambidexterity' to balance both long-term investment driven by consistent and stable policies with short-term responsiveness in the face of economic shocks. High-quality institutions leading to regional growth is a major policy priority (Rodríguez-Pose, 2020).

Selecting the right kinds of firms to both save and help grow is also essential. Those with high levels of embeddedness, creating strong local multipliers, help leverage limited public resources for maximum impact. This is the kind of informed precision that the policy regime needs to apply in promoting greater levels of local value appropriation, from stronger RIS. This in turn requires a more even distribution of public R&D funding and a focus on STEM assets to improve firm-level innovation and productivity. These can also help scale up SMEs and improve the skills of lower-skilled, lower-income workers as part of an inclusive RIS development strategy. Central to more effective RIS, there is significant potential in the commercialisation of a larger proportion of university-based R&D, better-leveraged to improve local firm-level productivity and innovation. A stronger RIS can also be used to support faster transitions to new growth sectors away from legacy industries. Finally, we also refer to the potential of public-sector procurement to help in this targeted approach to local development.

To reiterate, this requires a truly *regional* industrial strategy, taking account of the spatial dimensions of growth because current policy is 'sectorally narrow and spatially blind' (Fothergill et al., 2019). An industrial strategy based on inclusive innovation is contingent on a wider set of changes. It will not be achieved by incremental change because the scale of investment needed to rebuild infrastructure, boost education and skills, restructure public services and enable higher levels of productivity through stronger RIS is so great. In addition, the leap in political will and the gap in institutional governance structures from over-centralised to locally devolved is huge.

There are some lessons to be learned from China's experience, although outside the scope of this discussion. It operates a carefully managed top-down, bottom-up duality, with local contributions to a centralised policymaking structure, alongside long-term industrial strategies for balanced growth. Although it has achieved both economic growth and increased average incomes by an unprecedented amount over the past decades, there is still a long way to go, particularly in terms of income inequalities. But the Chinese Provinces are the deliberate focus of a partly competitive and partly experimental process of entrepreneurial policymaking. A consistent practice of developing five-year plans for economic and social development (since the 1950s) is maintained, and the planning for the fifteenth of these (2026–2030) started in 2023. Each time this involves a collective lessons-learned phase before further implementation, using empirical data and insights from across the country.

City-REDI is included in this Element as an example of one type of investment that can help rebalance the relative lack of data, local insights and policy intelligence in the UK context. It also points to the importance of coalitions of locally embedded organisations, including universities and representative business organisations, linked to national agencies. A final recommendation would be for a national competition to solicit multiple City-REDI-type proposals to support the development of local knowledge and agency, to capture lessons learned and fine-tune transformative projects that would attract public and private investment over the long term.

This is not just about spending public funding more effectively and efficiently. It is also more than a moral imperative to reduce inequality. Failure to address these serious socio-economic imbalances could fuel the kinds of mass discontent that have led to radical regime change and in some cases the end of civilisations, in other countries in other times. It will take a concerted effort by coalitions of the willing to transition to a new variety of inclusive capitalism in the UK and beyond.

References

Agrawal, S. and Phillips, D. (2020), *Catching Up or Falling Behind? Geographical Inequalities in the UK and How They Have Changed in Recent Years*, Institute for Fiscal Studies (IFS) Deaton Review, www.ifs.org.uk/inequality/geographical-inequalities-in-the-uk/.

Aitken, A., Foliano, F., Mariona, L. S. et al. (2021) From Ideas to Growth: Understanding the Drivers of Innovation and Productivity across Firms, Regions, and Industries in the UK. *BEIS Research Paper* 2021/041. https://dera.ioe.ac.uk/39017/1/niesr-report.pdf.

Bailey, D., Glasmeier, A., Tomlinson, P. R. and Tyler, P. (2019) Industrial Policy: New Technologies and Transformative Innovation Policies? *Cambridge Journal of Regions, Economy and Society*, 12(2), 169–177. https://doi.org/10.1093/cjres/rsz006.

Bailey, D., Pitelis, C. and Tomlinson, P. R. (2018) A Place-Based Developmental Regional Industrial Strategy for Sustainable Capture of Co-created Value. *Cambridge Journal of Economics*, 42(6), 1521–1542. https://doi.org/10.1093/cje/bey019.

Bailey, D., Pitelis, C. N. and Tomlinson, P. R. (2023) Place-Based Industrial and Regional Strategy – Levelling the Playing Field. *Regional Studies*, 57(6), 977–983. https://doi.org/10.1080/00343404.2023.2168260.

Balland, P. A., Boschma, R., Crespo, J. and Rigby, D. (2019) Smart Specialization Policy in the EU: Relatedness, Knowledge Complexity and Regional Diversification. *Regional Studies*, 53(9), 1252–1268. https://doi.org/10.1080/00343404.2018.1437900.

Balland, P.-A., Broekel, T., Diodato, D. et al. (2022) The New Paradigm of Economic Complexity. *Research Policy*, 51, 8. https://doi.org/10.1016/j.respol.2022.104568.

Bauluz, L., Bukowski, P., Fransham, M. et al. (2023) Spatial Wage Inequality in North America and Western Europe: Changes between and Within Local Labour Markets 1975-2019. *World Inequality Lab –, Kiel Working Paper* (No. 2253). https://www.econstor.eu/handle/10419/274019.

Becker, B., Roper, S. and Vanino, E. (2023) Assessing Innovation Spillovers from Publicly Funded R&D and Innovation Support: Evidence from the UK. *Technovation*, 128, 102860. https://doi.org/10.1016/j.technovation.2023.102860.

Behringer, J. and van Treeck, T. (2022) Varieties of capitalism and growth regimes: the role of income distribution. *Socio-Economic Review*, 20(3), 1249–1286, https://doi.org/10.1093/ser/mwab032.

Belso-Martinez, J. A., Díez-Vial, I. and Rodríguez-Pose, A. (2024) Inter-organizational Governance and Innovation under Different Local Institutional Contexts. *Journal of Economic Geography*, 24(4), 527–548. https://doi.org/10.1093/jeg/lbae001.

Bento, N., Sousa, C., Trindade, P. et al. (2022) Robust Relation between Public Procurement for Innovation and Economic Development. *Economics Letters*, 211, 110241. https://doi.org/10.1016/j.econlet.2021.110241.

Bianchi, N, Giorcelli, M, Martino, E. M. (2023) The Effects of Fiscal Decentralisation on Publicly Provided Services and Labour Market. *Economic Journal*, 133(653), 1738–1772. https://doi.org/10.1093/ej/uead022.

Billing, C., Bramley, G., Ioramashvili, C. et al. (2023) The Impact of University STEM Assets: A Systematic Review of the Empirical Evidence. *PLoS ONE*, 18(6), e0287005. https://doi.org/10.1371/journal.pone.0287005.

Billing, C., Bryson, J. R. and Kitsos, T. (2024) Industrial Path Development in the UK Space Sector: Processes of Legitimacy Building in the Establishment of Space 2.0. *Industry and Innovation*, 31(8), 945–970. https://doi.org/10.1080/13662716.2024.2305865.

Billing, C., Collinson, S. C., Pan, F., Green, A. and Cepeda-Zorrilla, M. (2020) Which kinds of firms contribute most to regional growth? *City-REDI Policy Briefing Series*, University of Birmingham. https://blog.bham.ac.uk/cityredi/city-redi-policy-briefing-which-kinds-of-firms-contribute-most-to-regional-growth/.

Billing, C., McCann, P. and Ortega-Argilés, R. (2019) Interregional Inequalities and UK Sub-national Governance Responses to Brexit. *Regional Studies*, 53(5), 741–760. https://doi.org/10.1080/00343404.2018.1554246.

Blöchliger, H. and Akgun, O. (2018) Fiscal Decentralisation and Economic Growth. in Kim, J. and Dougherty, S. (eds.), *Fiscal Decentralisation and Inclusive Growth*, Paris: OECD publishing, 25–47. https://doi.org/10.1787/9789264302488-4-en.

Blundell, R., Cribb, J., McNally, S., Warwick, R., and Xu, X. (2021) *Inequalities in Education, Skills, and Incomes in the UK: The Implications of the COVID-19 Pandemic*. London: IFS. https://ifs.org.uk/publications/inequalities-education-skills-and-incomes-uk-implications-covid-19-pandemic.

Blundell, R., Costa Dias, M., Joyce, R. and Xu, X. (2020) COVID-19 and Inequalities, *Fiscal Studies*, 41, 291–319.

References

Bramley G, Pugh, A. and Schwarz J. (2021) *Evaluation of the GBSLEP Pivot & Prosper Grant Fund Programme. Final Report.* https://gbslep.co.uk/resource/report/pivot-prosperevaluation-report.

Brown, A. (2023) How To Unlock Green and Place-Based Public Investment With the Help of HM Treasury's Green Book and Systems Thinking in Economics, *City-REDI blog*. 10 August 2023. https://blog.bham.ac.uk/cityredi/how-to-unlock-green-and-place-based-public-investment-with-the-help-of-hm-treasurys-green-book-and-systems-thinking-in-economics/.

Carrascal Incera, A., Kitsos, A. and Gutierrez Posada, D. (2022) Universities, Students and Regional Economies: A Symbiotic Relationship? *Regional Studies*, 56(6), 892–908, https://doi.org/10.1080/00343404.2021.1925236.

Carrascal-Incera, A., McCann, P., Ortega-Argilés, R. and Rodríguez-Pose, A. (2020) UK Interregional Inequality in a Historical and International Comparative Context. *National Institute Economic Review*, 253, R4–R17. https://doi.org/10.1017/nie.2020.26.

Ciarli, T., Marzucchi, A., Salgado, E. and Savona, M. (2018) The effect of R&D growth on employment and self-employment in local labour markets. *SPRU, University of Sussex Report.* https://hdl.handle.net/10779/uos.23476460.v1.

CLES. (2018) *Local Wealth Building in Birmingham and Beyond*, The Centre for Local Economic Strategies, https://cles.org.uk/publications/local-wealth-building-in-birmingham-and-beyond/.

Collinson, S. C. (2023) Universities Role in Helping Regions Transition from Legacy Industries into New Areas, *City-REDI blog*, University of Birmingham. https://blog.bham.ac.uk/cityredi/universities-role-in-helping-regions-transition-from-legacy-industries-into-new-areas/.

Collinson, S. C. (2022) Providing the Right Support for the Right Firms in the Right Places, *City-REDI Blog*, University of Birmingham. https://blog.bham.ac.uk/cityredi/providing-the-right-support-for-the-right-firms-in-the-right-places/.

Collinson, S. C. (2020) (Ed.) *Informing Development of the UK Place-based R&D Strategy.* Research England/UKRI and WMREDI expert evidence forum report. University of Birmingham. www.birmingham.ac.uk/documents/college-social-sciences/business/research/wm-redi/wmredi-ukri-rd-forum-report-full.pdf.

Collinson, S., Driffield, N., Hoole, C., and Kitsos, A. (2022) Between a Rock and a Hard Place: Trade-offs between Prosperity and Inclusivity When Implementing Regional Growth Policies, *Productivity Insights Paper* No. 013, The Productivity Institute, University of Manchester.

Collinson, S. C., Hoole, C., and Newman, J. (2023a) England's Catch-22: Institutional Limitations to Achieving Balanced Growth through Devolution,

Journal of Contemporary Social Science, 18(3–4), 428–448. https://doi.org/10.1080/21582041.2023.2203122.

Collinson, S. C., Lyons, M. and Ma, H. (2023b) The Poorest UK Households are Hit Hardest by the Highest Rate of Firm Failure, *City-REDI Blog*, University of Birmingham. https://blog.bham.ac.uk/cityredi/the-poorest-uk-households-are-hit-hardest-by-the-highest-rate-of-firm-failure/.

Collinson, S. C., Kitagawa, F. and Ulrichsen, T. (2024a) Enhancing University Contributions to Local Growth by Targeting High-Potential Firms and Industries, *City-REDI Blog*, University of Birmingham. https://blog.bham.ac.uk/cityredi/enhancing-university-contributions-to-local-growth-by-targeting-high-potential-firms-and-industries/.

Collinson, S. C., Kitagawa, F. and Ulrichsen, T. (2024b) Place Matters: Universities and Local Innovation Systems, *City-REDI Blog*, University of Birmingham. https://blog.bham.ac.uk/cityredi/place-matters-universities-and-local-innovation-systems/.

Coyle, D. (2023) Economic Progress and Adam Smith's Dilemma. *National Institute Economic Review*, 265, 5–11. https://doi.org/10.1017/nie.2023.21.

Coyle, D. and Muhtar, A. (2023) Levelling Up Policies and the Failure to Learn. *Contemporary Social Science*, 18(3–4), 406–427. https://doi.org/10.1080/21582041.2023.2197877.

Coyle, D., and Sensier, M. (2020) The Imperial Treasury: Appraisal Methodology and Regional Economic Performance in the UK. *Regional Studies*, 54(3), 283–295.

Coyle, D., van Ark, B. and Pendrill, J. (eds.) (2023) *The Productivity Agenda. Report No. 001*. Manchester: The Productivity Institute, The University of Manchester.

Crafts, N. (2009) Transport Infrastructure Investment: Implications for Growth and Productivity. *Oxford Review of Economic Policy*, 25(3), 327–343. https://doi.org/10.1093/oxrep/grp021.

Davenport, A. and Zaranko, B. (2020) *Levelling Up: Where and How?* in Bourquin, P., Johnson, A., Smith, B. et al. (eds.), *IFS Green Budget 2020*, London: Institute for Fiscal Studies, 315–372. www.ifs.org.uk/publications/15055.

Deleidi, M. and Mazzucato, M. (2021) Directed Innovation Policies and the Supermultiplier: An Empirical Assessment of Mission-Oriented Policies in the US Economy. *Research Policy*, 50(2), 104151. https://doi.org/10.1016/j.respol.2020.104151.

Denning, S. and Hastings, H. (2024) *Aberrant Capitalism: The Decay and Revival of Customer Capitalism*. Elements in Reinventing Capitalism series. Cambridge: Cambridge University Press.

Dorling, D. (2023) *Shattered Nation: Inequality and the Geography of a Failing State*. London: Verso, ISBN- 13: 978-1-80429-327-0.

Drayton, E., Farquharson, C, Ogden, K. et al. (2024) *Annual Report on Education Spending in England: 2023*. London: IFS. https://ifs.org.uk/publications/annual-report-education-spending-england-2023.

DSIT (2024) *Introducing the Innovation Clusters Map*, Statement from the Secretary of State, Department for Science, Innovation, and Technology, UK Government. www.gov.uk/government/speeches/introducing-the-innovation-clusters-map.

Dunford, M. (2022) The Chinese Path to Common Prosperity. *International Critical Thought*, 12(1), 35–54. https://doi.org/10.1080/21598282.2022.2025561.

Eatwell, R. and Goodwin, M. (2018) *National Populism: The Revolt against Liberal Democracy*. London: Penguin Books.

Ezcurra, R. and Rodríguez-Pose, A. (2013) Political Decentralization, Economic Growth and Regional Disparities in the OECD. *Regional Studies*, 47(3), 388–401.

Flanagan, K., Uyarra, E. and Wanzenböck, I. (2023) Towards a Problem-Oriented Regional Industrial Policy: Possibilities for Public Intervention in Framing, Valuation and Market Formation. *Regional Studies*, 57(6), 998–1010. https://doi.org/10.1080/00343404.2021.2016680.

Forth, T. (2023) *Levelling Up: Another Decade of Not Trying*. Leeds: Tom Forth publications. https://tomforth.co.uk/stillnottrying/ (04 October 2023).

Forth, T. and Jones, R. (2020) *The Missing £4 Billion: Making R&D Work for the Whole UK*, Nesta. www.nesta.org.uk/report/the-missing-4-billion/.

Fothergill, S., Gore, T. and Wells, P. (2019) Industrial Strategy and the UK Regions: Sectorally Narrow and Spatially Blind. *Cambridge Journal of Regions, Economy and Society*, 12, 445–466.

Fransham, M., Herbertson, M., Pop, M., Bandeira Morais, M. and Lee, N. (2023) Level Best? The Levelling Up Agenda and UK Regional Inequality. *Regional Studies*, 57(11), 2339–2352.

Geary, F. and Stark, T. (2016) What Happened to Regional Inequality in Britain in the Twentieth Century? *Economic History Review*, 69, 215–228.

Gibbons, S., Overman, H. and Pelkonen, P. (2013) Area Disparities in Britain: Understanding the Contribution of People vs. Place Through Variance Decompositions. *Oxford Bulletin of Economics and Statistics*, 76, 1–19.

Gómez-Tello, A., Murgui-García, M. J. and Sanchis-Llopis, M. T. (2020) Exploring the Recent Upsurge in Productivity Disparities between European Regions. *Growth and Change*, 51, 1491–1516. https://doi.org/10.1111/grow.12414.

Green, A. (2023) *When should place-based policies be used and at what scale?* OECD-EC High-Level Expert Workshop Series on 'Place-Based Policies for the Future', Workshop 2, 12 May 2023. www.oecd.org/cfe/regionaldevelopment/place-based-policies-for-thefuture.htm.

Griffith, R., Huergo, E., Mairesse, J. and Peters, B. (2006) Innovation and Productivity Across Four European Countries. *Oxford Review of Economic Policy*, 22(4), 483–498. https://doi.org/10.1093/oxrep/grj028.

Hall P. A. and Gingerich D. W. (2009) Varieties of Capitalism and Institutional Complementarities in the Political Economy: An Empirical Analysis. *British Journal of Political Science*, 39(3), 449–482. https://doi.org/10.1017/S0007123409000672.

Hall, P. A. and Soskice, D. (eds.) (2001) *Varieties of Capitalism: The Institutional Foundations of Comparative Advantage*. Oxford: Oxford University Press.

Hansen, T. (2022) The Foundational Economy and Regional Development. *Regional Studies*, 56, 1033–1042.

Hart, M. (2023) Business Support Re-Organisation in England at a Time of Crisis, *City-REDI blog*, University of Birmingham. https://blog.bham.ac.uk/cityredi/business-support-re-organisation-in-england-at-a-time-of-crisis/.

Hausman, N. (2022) University Innovation, Local Economic Growth, and Entrepreneurship. *Review of Economics and Statistics*, 104, 718–735.

Hausmann, R., Klinger, B., and Wagner, R. (2008) Doing Growth Diagnostics in Practice: A 'Mindbook', *CID Working Paper Series*.

Hausmann, R., Rodrik, D., and Velasco, A. (2008) Growth Diagnostics, in Serra, N. and Stiglitz, J. E. (eds.), *The Washington Consensus Reconsidered: Towards a New Global Governance*, Oxford: Oxford Academic, 324–355. https://doi.org/10.1093/acprof:oso/9780199534081.003.0015.

Holmes Jr., R. M., Waldman, D. A., Siegel, D. S. and Pepe, J. A. (2022) Declining Trust in Capitalism: Managerial, Research, and Public Policy Implications. *AMP*, 36, 984–1006, https://doi.org/10.5465/amp.2021.0011.

Hudson, P. and Tribe, K. (eds.). (2017) *The Contradictions of Capital in the Twenty-First Century: The Piketty Opportunity*. New York: Columbia University Press.

Iammarino, S., Rodriguez-Pose, A and Storper, M. (2019) Regional Inequality in Europe: Evidence, Theory and Policy Implications. *Journal of Economic Geography*, 19(2), 273–298.

Ioramashvili, C., Lynam, R., Billing, C. and Collinson, S.C. (2022a) The Manufacturing Technology Centre, *WMREDI Policy Briefing*. https://blog

.bham.ac.uk/cityredi/wmredi-policy-briefing-the-manufacturing-technology-centre/.

Ioramashvili, C., Collinson, S. C., Humphreys, K., Read, H. and Pan, F. (2022b) Regional Systems of Innovation – How Does the West Midlands Compare With its European Counterparts? *City-REDI Blog*, University of Birmingham. https://blog.bham.ac.uk/cityredi/regional-systems-of-innovation-how-does-the-west-midlands-compare-with-its-european-counterparts/.

Jibril, H., Roper, S. and Ortega-Argiles, R. (2024) A General Framework for Innovation and Commercialisation Infrastructure for Emerging Technologies. *UK Innovation and Research Caucus Report* 002. https://ircaucus.ac.uk/publications/a-general-framework-for-innovation-and-commercialisation-infrastructure-for-emerging-technologies/.

Johnston, A., Wells, P., & Woodhouse, D. (2022) Examining the Roles of Universities in Place-Based Industrial Strategy: Which Characteristics Drive Knowledge Creation in Priority Technologies? *Regional Studies*, 1, 12. https://doi.org/10.1080/00343404.2021.1956683.

JRF (2024) *UK Poverty 2024*, The Joseph Rowntree Foundation. www.jrf.org.uk/uk-poverty-2024-the-essential-guide-to-understanding-poverty-in-the-uk?trk=public_post_comment-text.

Kantor, S. and Whalley, A. (2014) Knowledge Spillovers from Research Universities: Evidence from Endowment Value Shocks. *Review of Economics and Statistics*, 96(1), 171–188. https://doi.org/10.1162/REST_a_00357.

Kemeny, T. and Storper, M. (2023) The Changing Shape of Spatial Income Disparities in the United States. *Economic Geography*, 100(1), 1–30. https://doi.org/10.1080/00130095.2023.2244111.

Kitagawa, F. (2024) Universities' Role in Helping Regions Transition From Legacy Industries Into New Areas, *City-REDI Blog*, University of Birmingham. https://blog.bham.ac.uk/cityredi/universities-role-in-helping-regions-transition-from-legacy-industries-into-new-areas/.

Kitsos, T., Grabner, S. M. and Carrascal-Incera, A. (2023) Industrial Embeddedness and Regional Economic Resistance in Europe. *Economic Geography*, 99(3), 227–252. https://doi.org/10.1080/00130095.2023.2174514.

Lavie, D. (2023) *The Cooperative Economy: A Solution to Societal Grand Challenges*. London: Routledge.

Lee, N. (2024) *Innovation for the Masses: How to Share the Benefits of the High-Tech Economy*. Oakland, CA: University of California Press, ISBN 9780520394889.

Lee, N. (2023) Inclusive Innovation in Cities: From Buzzword to Policy. *Regional Studies*, https://doi.org/10.1080/00343404.2023.2168637.

London Economics (2024) *The Economic Impact of the Russell Group Universities' R&D Activities*. Final Report for the Russell Group, January 2024, https://russellgroup.ac.uk/policy/policy-documents/economic-impact-of-research-and-commercialisation-activities/.

London Economics (2023) *Cambridge University's Economic Impact*. Final Report for the University of Cambridge. www.cam.ac.uk/stories/cambridge-economic-impact.

London Economics (2021) *The economic impact of the University of Oxford*. Final Report for the University of Oxford. www.ox.ac.uk/research/recognition/economic-impact.

Lumpkin, G. T., Meléndez, E. and Bacq, S. (2024) Civic Wealth Creation: Bypassing Monopolies through Collective Action. *Academy of Management Perspectives*, 38, 165–176, https://doi.org/10.5465/amp.2022.0105.

Lyons, M., Ma, H. and Collinson, S. C. (2025) Better policies to mitigate the negative impacts of firm insolvencies on households and regional resilience, *City-REDI Working Paper*. City-REDI, University of Birmingham.

Marquis, C. (2024) *The Profiteers: How Business Privatizes Profits and Socializes Costs*. New York: PublicAffairs Publishing. ISBN 1541703545.

Marquis, C. (2020) *Better Business: How the B Corp Movement is Remaking Capitalism*. New Haven: Yale University Press.

Martin, R., Gardiner, B., Pike, A., Sunley, P. and Tyler, P. (2021) *Levelling up Left Behind Places: The Scale and Nature of the Economic and Policy Challenge*. London: Routledge.

Martin, R., Sunley, P., Gardiner, B., Evenhuis, E. and Tyler, P. (2018) The City Dimension of the Productivity Problem: The Relative Role of Structural Change and Within-Sector Slowdown. *Journal of Economic Geography*, 18(3), 539–570.

Martynovich, M., Hansen, T. and Lundquist, K.-J. (2023) Can Foundational Economy Save Regions in Crisis? *Journal of Economic Geography*, 23(3), 577–599, https://doi.org/10.1093/jeg/lbac027.

Mazzucato, M. (2020) Mission-Oriented Public Procurement: Lessons from International Examples. *UCL Institute for Innovation and Public Purpose, Policy Report*, (IIPP WP 2020-20). www.ucl.ac.uk/bartlett/public-purpose/wp2020-20.

Mazzucato, M. (2021) *Mission Economy: A Moonshot Guide to Changing Capitalism*. London: Allen Lane.

Mazzucato, M. and Perez, C. (2023) Redirecting Growth: Inclusive, Sustainable and Innovation-Led, in Reinert, E. S. and Kvangraven, I. H. (eds.), *A Modern Guide to Uneven Economic Development*, Cheltenham, UK: Edward Elgar, 71–106.

McCann, P. (2016) *The UK Regional-National Economic Problem: Geography, Globalisation and Governance* (1st ed.). London: Routledge. https://doi.org/10.4324/9781315627151.

McCann, P. (2020) Perceptions of Regional Inequality and the Geography of Discontent: Insights from the UK. *Regional Studies*, 54(2), 256–267. https://doi.org/10.1080/00343404.2019.1619928.

McCann, P. and Ortega-Argilés, R. (2021) The UK 'Geography of Discontent': Narratives, Brexit and Inter-Regional 'Levelling Up'. *Cambridge Journal of Regions, Economy and Society*, 14(3), 545–564. https://doi.org/10.1093/cjres/rsab017.

McCann, P., Ortega-Argilés, R., Sevinc, D. and Cepeda-Zorrilla, M. (2021) Rebalancing UK Regional and Industrial Policy Post-Brexit and Post-COVID-19: Lessons Learned and Priorities for the Future. *Regional Studies*, 57(6), 1113–1125. https://doi.org/10.1080/00343404.2021.1922663.

McCann, P. and Yuan, P.-Y. (2022) The Productivity Performance of Different Types of UK Regions and the Challenges of Levelling Up. *National Institute Economic Review*, 261, 79–98. https://doi.org/10.1017/nie.2022.24.

Mealy, P. and Coyle, D., (2022) To Them That Hath: Economic Complexity and Local Industrial Strategy in the UK. *International Tax and Public Finance*, 29(2), 358–377.

Moretti, E., Steinwender, C. and Van Reenen, J. (2019) The Intellectual Spoils of War? Defense R&D, Productivity and International Spillovers. *National Bureau of Economic Research. NBER Working Paper 26483*. www.nber.org/papers/w26483.

Morgan, K. (2019) The Future of Place-Based Innovation Policy (As If 'Lagging Regions' Really Mattered), in Barzotto, M., Corradini, C., Fai, F. M., Labory, S., and Tomlinson, P. R. (eds.), *Revitalising Lagging Regions: Smart Specialisation and Industry 4.0*, London: Routledge, 79–90.

Movahed, M. (2023) Varieties of Capitalism and Income Inequality. *International Journal of Comparative Sociology*, 64(6), 621–657. https://doi.org/10.1177/00207152231174158.

Nafizah, Y. U. and Roper, S. (2024) *How Well Do Barriers and Enablers Predict Regional Innovation? Evidence from the Innovation State of the Nation 2023*. Oxford: Innovation and Research Caucus. IRC Report 4. https://ircaucus.ac.uk/publications/how-well-do-barriers-and-enablers-predict-regional-innovation-evidence-from-the-innovation-state-of-the-nation-2023/.

Newman, J., Driffield, N., Collinson, S., Gilbert, N., and Hoole, C. (2023) Mechanisms of Metagovernance as Structural Challenges to Levelling Up in England. *Regional Studies*, 58(4), 876–892. www.tandfonline.com/doi/full/10.1080/00343404.2023.2217215.

OECD (2023a) *Subnational Governments in OECD Countries: Key Data, 2023*. Paris: OECD. www.oecd.org/regional/multi-level-governance/NUANCIER%202023-3.pdf.

OECD (2023b) Size of public procurement, Government at a Glance 2023, OECD iLibrary. www.oecd-ilibrary.org/sites/ce2208f6-en/index.html?itemId=/content/component/ce2208f6-en.

OECD (2024) *Reviving Broadly Shared Productivity Growth in Spain*. Paris: OECD. https://doi.org/10.1787/34061b21-en.

ONS (2022) *Household Total Wealth in Great Britain: April 2018 to March 2020*, Office for National Statistics bulletin. www.ons.gov.uk/peoplepopulationandcommunity/personalandhouseholdfinances/incomeandwealth/bulletins/totalwealthingreatbritain/april2018tomarch2020.

Overman, H. G. and Xu, X. (2022), Spatial disparities across labour markets, *IFS Deaton Review of Inequalities*. https://ifs.org.uk/inequality/wp-content/uploads/2022/02/Spatial-disparities-across-labour-markets-IFS-Deaton-Review-Inequality-FINAL.pdf.

Panjwani, A. (2023) Research and Development Spending, *House of Commons Library Research Briefing* (SN04223) (11/9/2023). https://researchbriefings.files.parliament.uk/documents/SN04223/SN04223.pdf.

Parke, C. (2021) Anchor Network Supply Chain Hub: A Proposal, *City-REDI Blog*, University of Birmingham. https://blog.bham.ac.uk/cityredi/anchor-network-supply-chain-hub-a-proposal/.

Pike, A., Rodríguez-Pose, A., and Tomaney, J. (2016) *Local and Regional Development*. Abingdon: Taylor and Francis.

Piketty, T. (2014) *Capital in the Twenty-First Century*. Cambridge, MA: The Belknap Press of Harvard University Press.

Piketty, T. (2020) *Capital and Ideology*. London: Harvard University Press.

Pinheiro, F. L., Balland, P.-A., Boschma, R. and Hartmann, D. (2022) The Dark Side of the Geography of Innovation: Relatedness, Complexity and Regional Inequality in Europe. *Regional Studies*, 59(1). 1-16. https://doi.org/10.1080/00343404.2022.2106362.

Public Health England (2024) *Health Profile for England 2021*. https://fingertips.phe.org.uk/static-reports/health-profile-for-england/hpfe_report.html.

Qamar, A., Collinson, S., and Green, A. (2022) Covid-19 Disruption, Resilience and Industrial Policy: The Automotive Sector in the West Midlands. *Regional Studies*, 57(6), 1156–1170. https://doi.org/10.1080/00343404.2022.2126449.

Redding, G. (2023) *Comparing Capitalisms for an Unknown Future: Societal Processes and Transformative Capacity*, Elements in Reinventing Capitalism series, published online by Cambridge University Press.

Riley, R., Collinson, S., Green, A. and Ortega-Argiles, R. (2022) The City-Region Economic Development Institute – Establishing a Successful Place-Based Research Institute to Support Regions in Turbulent Times and Beyond, in Vorley T., Rahman, S. A., Tuckerman, L. and Wallace, P. (eds.), *How to Engage Policy Makers with Your Research: The Art of Informing and Impacting Policy*, Cheltenham, UK: Edward Elgar, 196–206.

Rodríguez-Pose, A. (2020) Institutions and the fortunes of territories. *Regional Science Policy & Practice*, 12, 371–386. https://doi.org/10.1111/rsp3.12277.

Rodríguez-Pose, A. (2018) The Revenge of the Places That Don't Matter (and what to do about it). *Cambridge Journal of Regions, Economy and Society*, 11, 189–209.

Rodrigues, G. and Breach, A. (2021) *Measuring up: Comparing public transport in the UK and Europe's Biggest Cities*, Centre for Cities. www.centreforcities.org/wp-content/uploads/2021/11/Measuring-Up-Comparing-Public-Transport-in-the-UK-and-Europes-Biggest-Cities.pdf.

Rodrik, D. (2000) Institutions for High-Quality Growth: What They Are and How to Acquire Them," *Studies in Comparative International Development*, 35(3), 3–31.

Rodrik, D. and Sabel, C. F. (2019) Building a Good Jobs Economy, *Harvard Kennedy School Faculty Research Working Paper No. RWP20-001*. https://scholarship.law.columbia.edu/faculty_scholarship/2608

Rossi, F., Baines, N. and Lawton Smith, H. (2023) Which Regional Conditions Facilitate University Spinouts Retention and Attraction? *Regional Studies*, 57(6), 1096–1112, https://doi.org/10.1080/00343404.2021.1959909.

Rodríguez-Pose, A. and Muštra, V. (2022) The Economic Returns of Decentralisation: Government Quality and the Role of Space. *Environment and Planning A: Economy and Space*, 54(8), 1604–1622.

Salter, M. S. (2024) The Fading Light of Democratic Capitalism, Elements in Reinventing Capitalism series, published online by Cambridge University Press. www.cambridge.org/core/elements/abs/fading-light-of-democratic-capitalism/E8E90383468ABCBF7DCCAF2BBC9B9A7C.

Sensier, M., Rafferty, A. and Devine, F. (2023) The Economic Resilience Scorecard: Regional Policy Responses for Crises Recovery. *Regional Studies*, 58(9), 1754–1766. https://doi.org/10.1080/00343404.2023.2234950.

Social Mobility Commission (2020) *Research and Analysis: The Best and Worst Social Mobility Areas in England*. London: UK Government Digital

Services. www.gov.uk/government/publications/the-long-shadow-of-depriv ation-differences-in-opportunities/tables-best-and-worst-social-mobility- areas-in-england.

Stansbury, A., Turner, D. and Balls, E. (2023) Tackling the UK's Regional Economic Inequality: Binding Constraints and Avenues for Policy Intervention, Mossavar-Rahmani Center for Business & Government. *Associate Working Paper Series, No. 198, Harvard Kennedy School*, and *Contemporary Social Science*, 18(3–4), 318–356, https://doi.org/10.1080/ 21582041.2023.2250745.

Sullivan, B., Hays, D. and Bennett, N. (2023) *The Wealth of Households: 2021*, Current Population Reports, P70BR-183, Washington, DC: U.S. Census Bureau.

Taylor, A. (2022) How Can the UK Learn From International Experience to Level Up? Drawing on Research from the Industrial Strategy Council, in Atherton, G. and Webb, C. (eds.), *Levelling Up: What Is It and Can It Work?* London: Centre for Inequality and Levelling Up (CEILUP), The University of West London, 15–17.

Thwaites, G. and Try, L. (2023) *Ending Stagnation: Technical Annex*, Resolution Foundation, December 2023. https://economy2030.resolutionfoundation.org/ wp-content/uploads/2023/12/FinalReport-TechnicalAnnex.pdf.

Tilley, H., Newman, J., Connell, A., Hoole, C. and Mukherjee, A. (2023) A Place-Based System? Regional Policy Levers and the UK's Productivity Challenge. *Regional Studies*, 57(10), 2102–2114, https://doi.org/ 00343404.2022.2152436.

Tomaney, J. and Pike, A. (2020) Levelling Up? *The Political Quarterly*, 91, 43–48.

Ulrichsen, T. C. and Roupakia, Z. (2024) *Spinning out Success: Demystifying UK university spinout trends, equity and investment*, Policy Evidence Unit for University Commercialisation and Innovation (UCI), University of Cambridge.

Uyarra, E., Zabala-Iturriagagoitia, J. M., Flanagan, K. and Magro, E. (2020) Public procurement, innovation and industrial policy: Rationales, roles, capabilities and implementation. *Research Policy*, 49(1), 103844. https:// doi.org/10.1016/j.respol.2019.103844.

van Ark, B., de Vries, K. and Pilat, D. (2024) Are pro-productivity policies fit for purpose? *The Manchester School*, 92(2), 191–208. https://doi.org/ 10.1111/manc.12464.

Vasilakos, N., Pitelis, A.T., Horsewood, N. and Pitelis, C. (2023) Place-based public investment in regional infrastructure, the locational choice of firms and regional performance: The case of India. *Regional Studies*, 57(6), 1055–1068. https://doi.org/10.1080/00343404.2022.2146666.

Westwood, A., Sensier, M. and Pike, N. (2022) The politics of levelling up: Devolution, institutions and productivity in England. *National Institute Economic Review*, 261, 99–116. https://doi.org/10.1017/nie.2022.29.

Wolf, M. (2023) *The Crisis of Democratic Capitalism*. London: Allen Lane, ISBN 978-0-241-30341-2, hardback.

Zymek, R. and Jones, B. (2020) UK Regional Productivity Differences: An Evidence Review. *Report for the Industrial Strategy Council*. https://industrialstrategycouncil.org/sites/default/files.

Cambridge Elements

Reinventing Capitalism

Arie Y. Lewin
Duke University

Arie Y. Lewin is Professor Emeritus of Strategy and International Business at Duke University, Fuqua School of Business. He is an Elected Fellow of the Academy of International Business and a Recipient of the Academy of Management inaugural Joanne Martin Trailblazer Award. Previously, he was Editor-in-Chief of *Management and Organization Review* (2015–2021) and the *Journal of International Business Studies* (2000–2007), founding Editor-in-Chief of Organization Science (1989–2007), and Convener of Organization Science Winter Conference (1990–2012). His research centers on studies of organizations' adaptation as co-evolutionary systems, the emergence of new organizational forms, and adaptive capabilities of innovating and imitating organizations. His current research focuses on de-globalization and decoupling, the Fourth Industrial Revolution, and the renewal of capitalism.

Till Talaulicar
University of Erfurt

Till Talaulicar holds the Chair of Organization and Management at the University of Erfurt where he is also the Dean of the Faculty of Economics, Law and Social Sciences. His main research expertise is in the areas of corporate governance and the responsibilities of the corporate sector in modern societies. Professor Talaulicar is Editor-in-Chief of *Corporate Governance: An International Review*, Senior Editor of Management and Organization Review and serves on the Editorial Board of Organization Science. Moreover, he has been Founding Member and Chairperson of the Board of the International Corporate Governance Society (2014–2020).

Editorial Advisory Board

Paul S. Adler, *University of Southern California, USA*
Ruth V. Aguilera, *Northeastern University, USA*
Christina Ahmadjian, *Hitotsubashi University, Japan*
Helena Barnard, *University of Pretoria, South Africa*
Jay Barney, *University of Utah, USA*
Jerry Davis, *University of Michigan, USA*
Steve Denning, *Forbes*
Rebecca Henderson, *Harvard University, USA*
Thomas Hutzschenreuter, *TU München, Germany*
Tarun Khanna, *Harvard University, USA*
Peter G. Klein, *Baylor University, USA*
Costas Markides, *London Business School, UK*
Anita McGahan, *University of Toronto, Canada*
Rita McGrath, *Columbia University, USA*
Heather McGregor, *Edinburgh Business School, UK*
Alan Meyer, *University of Oregon, USA*
Katrin Muff, *LUISS University Rome, Italy*
Peter Murmann, *University of St. Gallen, Switzerland*

Tsuyoshi Numagami, *Hitotsubashi University, Japan*
Margit Osterloh, *University of Basel, Switzerland*
Andreas Georg Scherer, *University of Zurich, Switzerland*
Blair Sheppard, *PwC, USA*
Jeffrey Sonnenfeld, *Yale University, USA*
John Sutton, *LSE, UK*
David Teece, *UC Berkeley, USA*
Anne S. Tsui, *University of Notre Dame, USA*
Alain Verbeke, *University of Calgary, Canada*
Henk Volberda, *University of Amsterdam, The Netherlands*
Mira Wilkins, *Florida International University, USA*
Sarah Williamson, *FCLTGlobal, USA*
Arjen van Witteloostuijn, *VU Amsterdam, The Netherlands*
George Yip, *Imperial College London, UK*

About the Series

This series seeks to feature explorations about the crisis of legitimacy facing capitalism today, including the increasing income and wealth gap, the decline of the middle class, threats to employment due to globalization and digitalization, undermined trust in institutions, discrimination against minorities, global poverty and pollution. Being grounded in a business and management perspective, the series incorporates contributions from multiple disciplines on the causes of the current crisis and potential solutions to renew capitalism.

Panmure House is the final and only remaining home of Adam Smith, Scottish philosopher and 'Father of modern economics.' Smith occupied the House between 1778 and 1790, during which time he completed the final editions of his master works: The Theory of Moral Sentiments and The Wealth of Nations. Other great luminaries and thinkers of the Scottish Enlightenment visited Smith regularly at the House across this period. Their mission is to provide a world-class twenty-first-century centre for social and economic debate and research, convening in the name of Adam Smith to effect positive change and forge global, future-focussed networks.

Cambridge Elements

Reinventing Capitalism

Elements in the Series

Reinventing Capitalism in the Digital Age
Stephen Denning

From Financialisation to Innovation in UK Big Pharma: AstraZeneca and GlaxoSmithKline
Öner Tulum, Antonio Andreoni, and William Lazonick

Comparing Capitalisms for an Unknown Future: Societal Processes and Transformative Capacity
Gordon Redding

The Future of Work in Diverse Economic Systems: The Varieties of Capitalism Perspective
Daniel Friel

Transforming our Critical Systems: How Can We Achieve the Systemic Change the World Needs?
Gerardus van der Zanden and Rozanne Henzen

Aberrant Capitalism: The Decay and Revival of Customer Capitalism
Hunter Hastings and Stephen Denning

Private Equity and the Demise of the Local: The Loss of Community Economic Power and Autonomy
Maryann Feldman and Martin Kenney

The Transformation of Boeing from Technological Leadership to Financial Engineering and Decline
Charles McMillan

The Fading Light of Democratic Capitalism: How Pervasive Cronyism and Restricted Suffrage Are Destroying Democratic Capitalism as a National Ideal . . .And What To Do About It
Malcolm S. Salter

Financing for Development: The Global Agenda
José Antonio Ocampo

State-Owned Enterprises as Institutional Actors in Contemporary Capitalism and Beyond
Olivier Butzbach, Douglas B. Fuller, Gerhard Schnyder and Luda Svystunova

Towards More Inclusive Varieties of Capitalism
Simon Collinson

A full series listing is available at: www.cambridge.org/RECA

For EU product safety concerns, contact us at Calle de José Abascal, 56–1°,
28003 Madrid, Spain or eugpsr@cambridge.org.